After my salutation to the French officer, things went very smoothly because he would slowly repeat everything I said in perfect French with more details, and most of the time I would simply say, "Oui, oui, c'est ca" (meaning "Yes, yes, that's right") or "Pas exactement" (meaning "Not exactly") and the good Capitaine would embellish or correct my French and we would be back to "Oui, oui, c'est ca."

Bob Caredi
5/26/21

The American Legacy
of an
Italian Motorcyclist

The American Legacy
of an
Italian Motorcyclist

Robert J. Paredi

Dedication

To Sandra Mary Weevers Paredi, my beautiful wife, who exhibited great forbearance as I undertook this book project, and to Catherine Ann Paredi and Jacqueline Gail Paredi, our beautiful daughters, who insisted for several years that I undertake the project.

Acknowledgments

Gianni Dametti, my Italian immigrant "Godfather"; Osborne Parker, my father's friend, classical record collector, and disc jockey; George Brenner, San Francisco Golden Gate music store manager and Daly City Orchestra Director; Miss French, Lick-Wilmerding H.S. English and French language professor; Mr. Tibbets, LWHS Chemistry and Earth Sciences professor; Orlando Giosi, San Francisco Symphony musician and my trumpet tutor; Nino Sechi, my neighbor and family friend; John Risso, my S.F. uncle, railway express mgr., WWII veteran, and summertime employer; Genis Mayolas, my Spanish step-grandfather; Thomas Patton, my Army buddy and witness to my introduction to my future bride, Sandra Weevers; Sheila Gazaleh, Sandra's sister; Henry Appen, my workmate and good friend, Creole Petroleum Corp., Maracaibo, Venezuela; Donald

Dreier, my friend and mentor, Maracaibo and EXXON Corp., EMCS Dept., NJ; Dick Biggs, fellow American PE, best friend and fishing pal in Venezuela, Truth or Consequences, NM; Mr. and Mrs. Rai Delacruz, my mother's elder-caretakers, Monterey, CA; Mr. and Mrs. Kenneth Pysher, my friends and literary supporters; Paulita Bennett-Martin, OCEANA-GA Coastal Region Program Director, my activist mentor; Mary Landers, *Savannah Morning News*, Letters to the Editor; and Liz Coursen, my editor and publisher.

Introduction

This book starts as an account of my Italian grandparents and parents immigrating to San Francisco, California, in the early 1900s. They came from diverse backgrounds: from poor and uneducated to economically successful and influential families. My maternal grandparents were escaping a hard life working as manager and housekeeper/cook in an Alsace-Lorraine boarding house—my grandfather arriving in San Francisco some months before my grandmother, who followed with my mother, an infant in arms, shortly after the city's devastating 1906 earthquake and fire. My father, the bemedaled young "Italian motorcyclist" of the book's title, elected to strike out on his own in America instead of joining his affluent family's generations-old silk manufacturing business in Italy.

The way my parents would meet in 1926 on a transatlantic crossing, fall in love, and marry within four months of meeting each other has all the ingredients of a Hollywood movie. Their eventual emigration back to San Francisco from northern Italy at the outset of the Great Depression was essentially forced upon them by the emergence of Mussolini's fascist nightmare. Had they remained in Italy and I had been born there instead of San Francisco, this book would never have been written. My parents' lives took several uncertain turns following their arrival in the States. The late 1920s and the entire decade of the 1930s marked a transformation in American civil society, which underwent the temporary madness of prohibition and the onset of the Great Depression, all accompanied by the permanent benefits deriving from the American women's suffrage movement. Every one of these events had a profound effect on the people in this story.

My book then goes on to describe my life, from boyhood through university, the military, marriage and family life, and corporate career, concluding in a surprisingly active retirement. My professional experiences gained in a career employed by the largest publicly owned oil corporation in the world led me to oppose the very activity in which I spent my professional life: petroleum engineering. The 12 years of oilfield operations in which I participated, in Venezuela and elsewhere, gave me a ringside seat in observing the pernicious effects of the petroleum industry upon our environment and lives. I hope that my experiences justify both my credibility and my hope of convincing you, my readers, to support scientifically based movements for a purposeful migration towards universal renewable energy sources.

My "accidental activism" in opposing petroleum exploration and production, one of the primary contributors to global warming and ocean degradation the world over, can no longer be described as the "pet peeve of tree-huggers" but as the worldwide consensus of the scientific community. In fact, there has finally emerged a convergence between worldwide progressive political actions and scientific sectors that defines the threat of fossil fuels to human civilization as "existential."

The American public's selection in 2020 of a new administration that believes in the sciences is a great relief. It lends significant hope that environmental threats to America and the world, such as global warming, rising ocean temperatures and levels, and undue reliance on fossil fuels are recognized and contained. The support of already apparent market-driven evolution to clean and renewable energy sources provides hope that future generations will not blame us for ignoring such threats to their lives.

My life was shaped by the remarkable personalities of my parents. Certain critical decisions they made while I, an only child, was growing up and being educated in the finest San

Francisco schools and U.C.-Berkeley had a profound effect on my life. I argued and resisted some of the decisions they seemed to have forced upon me at the time, from choices of schools to other seemingly trivial decisions. Many of those influential personal guidance decisions that good parents make on our behalf can appear contentious or trivial as we grow up. However, no doubt they influence whatever success or happiness we all enjoy when we are so lucky to have had parents who were subject to great challenges but overcame them, as my parents did.

—Bob Paredi, Savannah, Georgia, 2021

Table of Contents

Foreword to Bob's Book...................................1

1. No-Man's Land, 1915-1918........................7

2. The Immigrants....................................21

3. Eda's Secret Diary.................................29

4. The New Families..................................39

5. Erma's Idea..43

6. Making a Living...................................55

7. Growing Up..69

8. Dad's Breakthrough..............................97

9. Cleopatra's Victory Garden....................105

10. Italian Army POWs..............................115

11. Heroic Survivors.................................119

12. The Trumpeter...................................129

13. A Golden Opportunity..........................139

14. All Aboard!......................................149

15. The Story..157

16. My University Years............................165

17. Welcome to the Army............................177

18. Gobsmacked!.....................................195

19. Homecomings.....................................205

20. Welcome to Venezuela...........................213

21. Lessons from the Oil Patch.....................223

22. My Parents' Dream Move.........................243

23. My Dream Transfer..............................251

24. Return to America..............................263

25. Traveling, Headquarters Projects.............271

26. The Legacy Lives...............................283

27. Retirement.....................................289

28. The Accidental Activist.......................299

29. Devil's Bargain...............................323

30. Venezuela's Coda..............................327

Letters to the Editor............................333

1. MYTHS OF GEORGIA'S COASTLINE.........335

2. "FINDING OUT" MEANS DRILLING...........339

3. ATTACK ON GEORGIA'S COAST...............343

4. $66 BILLION AND COUNTING.................347

5. THE FIELD OF NIGHTMARES..................351

6. "ALL OF THE ABOVE" IS NO GOOD.........355

7. THANKS TO REP. CARTER.....................359

8. DOI PECCADILLO.................................363

9. LET THE OIL STAY THERE....................367

10. SUBSIDENCE, THE SLEEPING GIANT....369

11. WE MUST PROTECT OUR SHORES........371

12. OYSTERS & OIL DON'T MIX....................375

13. GOLDEN RAY SALVAGE CHALLENGE....377

14. FOSSIL FUEL INDUSTRY SKEWS CLEAN INDUSTRY FACTS...381

Additional Resources....................................383

Photo credits..385

Foreword to Bob's Book

—Dr. Richard O'Connor

I was surprised, yet very pleased, to be asked to write the Foreword to Bob Paredi's book. Surprised because I have just about run out of time to do this. To be blunt, I expect to enter a home hospice program within the week. I am embarrassed to admit that I completed a pretty well-edited draft; however, I lost it on my laptop. Yes, I overcame my pride and got some help. Unfortunately, it is a permanent loss, which for me is a double whammy. The first blow is the loss itself. The second blow is having to admit to myself how fast I am failing. Presently, I am reminding myself that I did catch a couple of breaks. First, I am not too uncomfortable, and second, I may be able to get my wife to type up this handwritten draft, though there is a small obstacle: we have a devil of a time reading each other's handwriting. Wow, I got an

1

extra special gift. My great-niece came to visit and bailed me out. She read through all my scribbled notes and helped me piece together this introduction.

I have known the author, Bob Paredi, for nearly 20 years. Candidly, I consider our friendship one of the really special gifts that I have received during my life. Bob has the ability to tell a good story, an interesting story without any embellishment of the facts or criticism of the participants. It may be helpful for you to know that I have always been impressed with the author's kindness and generosity, mixed with the broadness of his interests and the amazing array of his talents. I have worked on numerous projects with him without any tensions, or failures, which reflects both his adroit social skills and his vast mechanical abilities.

His is a very American story. To me, it is a very timely story, as it begins in 1917 after his father survives World War I and the 1918 pandemic is about to start. It is a very American story because Bob will be born to immigrant parents at the depth of the Great Depression, and whose comfort around foreign languages will have a profound effect on his early career as an engineer. The story details the complex relationships and patterns of immigrant families, as well as what motivates them to leave their country of origin. It also conveys the author's experiences growing up in San Francisco's

Italian immigrant community. His story is made even more interesting because of the large number of family photographs he was able to share with his publisher.

San Francisco was a very active port during World War II, and this created an opportunity for many immigrants, including Bob's father, to find employment. World War II also brought numbers of Italian war prisoners captured in the North Africa campaign to San Francisco. Eventually, Bob would spend his Sundays with his father driving around the Bay to the prisoner of war camp. His father would interview Italian prisoners in an effort to find information about Bob's uncle, who had been captured in Ethiopia around 1936.

It was during this time that Bob became a jazz aficionado and learned to play the trumpet. He was fortunate to be accepted to the well-known Lick Wilmerding High School in San Francisco, which later proved to be a steppingstone to his acceptance to the University of California-Berkeley, where he received his degree in engineering. While at Berkeley, Bob joined the ROTC and graduated as an officer. He very much wanted to be assigned to Europe and took the initiative to list his fluency in the languages of French, German, and Italian. He was assigned to an engineering battalion in France and upon completing his tour of duty he signed up to be a petroleum engineer on Lake Maracaibo in Venezuela.

Bob had always been interested in fishing, but it was when he had arrived in Venezuela that he began to indulge in his interests by fishing the headwaters of the Amazon. During his visits back to the States, he frequently fished the Russian River basin. Eventually, with a longtime friend, he would take pack horses into the upper reaches of Yosemite National Park to find incredible fishing opportunities. He has made several trips to the Bahamas to go bone fishing with a giant, nine-foot fly rod.

The platitude "Timing is everything" is better understood when one appreciates that a key determinant of the outcome is often *initiative*. In America, is it luck or necessity to be born to healthy parents? In America, is it luck or necessity to be born in a town where you will have access to an excellent public education? Is it luck or necessity for a male in America to turn 18 years old in a year without a war, a draft, a hometown riot, or a neighborhood disaster? Must he also be fair skinned to be safe enough to survive unscathed? This book helped me see that children of immigrants may want to marry other would-be immigrants, and it enhanced my appreciation of the breadth and depth of the contributions of immigrants and their offspring to the communities in which I have lived. The book led me to ponder why the tendency of contemporary Americans to participate in international travel makes most of them more tolerant and open minded, yet it disappoints me that a substantial segment of those with international travel experience remain wary, even suspicious, of foreigners.

At a time when a segment of America seems to devalue the contributions of immigrants to the robustness of our country, it is nice to have ready access to a story that shows quite clearly the contributions and success of first-generation Americans. For me it has special meaning because Bob and I grew up in a similar America during the same decades with overlapping interests, such as spending time outdoors in nature and working with our hands, building things. And to me, it is the unfinished story of the America in which I grew up, wending its way to an uncertain future.

Dr. Richard O'Connor (4/1/1941-9/3/2020)

The American Legacy of an Italian Motorcyclist

1. No-Man's Land, 1915-1918

Nino had just returned from the front lines of the Italian Army trenches on his American-made and -supplied Indian motorcycle to a scene of wild jubilation. He and his officer passenger, who jumped out of the bike's sidecar, joined the entire battalion of soldiers to celebrate that day, November 11, 1918, marking the Armistice of World War I, the supposed "war to end all wars."

My father, Giovanni "Nino" Paredi, had spent four years transporting infantry officers to and from the trenches to inspect the condition of their soldiers and their filthy and dangerous living conditions. On Nino's eighteenth birthday he had been inducted into the Italian Army Transportation Corps by the arrangement of his influential father, Ercole, who managed to prevent his eldest son from being drafted as an infantryman, unlikely to survive the brutal trench warfare on the Eastern Front of the conflict.

Nino's father, Ercole, age 19

The transportation battalion, which included Nino's motorcycle company, suffered occasional losses of large trucks loaded with supplies and/or Italian troops down the sides of steep mountains whose foot trails were not built for heavy truck traffic.

1. No-Man's Land, 1915-1918

1916 prima della ...
.... Cura

Nino the motorcyclist, age 19

The no-man's lands of that Austrian sector ranged from mountainous terrain to the foothills and plains of the Eastern Alps. Those plains, where hundreds of kilometers of zig-zagged trenches were dug, accounted for the highest mortality rates of

Austrian and Italian forces. The no-man's lands were defined as the areas between the respective troops' trenches and the lands behind them to the rear where their command posts, including medical services, were located. Like the front lines, these areas were also susceptible to the crudely aimed fire of incoming artillery, mortar, and gas attacks, which spared neither men nor beasts.

Nino with an officer in the sidecar of his Indian motorcycle

The motorcycle drivers quickly made a discovery: The motorcycles were practically impossible to safely steer over the ever-changing no-mans' lands without both hands constantly gripping the handlebar. The levers on each of the handlebar

1. No-Man's Land, 1915-1918

grips manually controlled the throttle, brakes, clutch, and gear box. A connecting rod linked the right-hand gear-shifting lever down to the small lever at the gear box by their right foot. By eliminating and discarding the connecting rod, operators learned to shift the gear box lever with their right foot. They were then able to shift gears while keeping both hands on the handlebar. This mechanical arrangement has been accepted as a standard by all motorcycle manufacturers since.

Nino's American-made Indian motorcycle was one of the nearly 50,000 motorcycles manufactured by the pioneering Indian Motorcycle company of Springfield, Massachusetts, for use by U.S. and allied forces in World War I. The company, which billed itself as "America's First Motorcycle Company," produced a lightweight, versatile, and maneuverable Indian bike that could be configured for such varied jobs as hauling a machine gun with a two-man crew (plus driver) or moving the wounded from the front via a one- or two-man sidecar ambulance. Metal wheels instead of rubber tires were added to a number of Indian bikes, so the bikes could be used on railroad tracks. The most common wartime use of a motorcycle, however, was as a reliable way to ferry officers to and from the front. This was Nino's responsibility. Nino's bike was often mounted with a single-passenger sidecar, as shown in the previous photo of Nino astride his Indian with an officer sitting in the sidecar. If you look closely at the cover photo, you'll see the word "Indian" on the front gas tank and, if you look even more closely, you can see the headlight and the tube where important dispatches and battlefield maps were carried for quick access. In fact, it looks as though there's a rolled up piece of paper in the tube at the moment this photo was taken! Other items Nino might have carried would have been medical supplies, ammunition, and gas tanks: the wartime Indian could be equipped with a rifle holder and folding brackets to secure large cans filled with gasoline and oil.

Nino and the men in his unit

Nino endured those four years of eating salami and hardtack (bullet-proof bread) and occasionally drinking bad wine. He had to urinate on his bike's

1. No-Man's Land, 1915-1918

windshield to melt the ice off in winters to improve his view. But he could not avert his eyes from the dangerous shell holes; the wounded, dying, or dead soldiers; the human and animal corpses littering the land. Nino navigated his motorcycle with its attached sidecar, with and without a passenger, over the constantly changing terrain. That no-man's land could dramatically change from hour to hour, night and day. Nino was justly awarded several medals, including the Croix de Guerre, for his exploits. He was safely reunited with his parents and younger siblings in far western Italy in the foothills of the Alps bordering France, the Piedmonte Region.

To the credit of his father and Nino's own luck and ingenuity, he returned a mature and respected 22-year-old veteran with the few other village comrades who survived the conflict.

Many years later Nino never dwelt in any detail on his harrowing war experiences with me, his son, Robert. However, while on duty Nino had acquired a large collection of postcards and some photographs throughout the Italian-Austrian Alps. No doubt Nino's experience in navigating safely through this dangerous terrain for four years prepared him to surmount the frequent challenges he would encounter for the rest of his life. That life was also heavily influenced by Europe's post-war dysfunction, particularly as the German National Socialist (Nazi) political party emerged under

Adolph Hitler's regime. Benito Mussolini was similarly inspired to lead Italy in the same direction. Nino had returned to a post-war Italy transformed from that of his boyhood to one that his family and younger siblings were suffering from, complaining about, but had to endure.

Returning from war, Nino initially considered continuing on with his family's traditional silk filature business. For three generations the Paredi family had owned and operated a silk filature factory. Being the first-born male of four children, custom would practically require that he do so.

The process of silk manufacture goes like this: Silkworm farmers collect millions of silkworms and feed them mulberry leaves gathered from neighboring natural forests or cultivations. After several intermediate stages, the silk filature factories receive the cocoons produced by the worms and start the process of extracting extremely fine fibers of silk, which are wound into stronger threads of 300 to 600 meters in length to produce a skein of silk thread. Quantities of the skeins are then packed into 60-kilo bales and shipped to fabric manufacturers.

Nino's family's business in silk filature production was being challenged by China. The Great Depression in the U.S. was on the near horizon.

I have a photo of an oil-painted portrait of Nino's great-grandfather, Ercole, followed by a photo of

1. No-Man's Land, 1915-1918

Nino's grandfather, Giovanni, followed by a photo of Nino's father, Ercole, followed by Nino's photo, followed by a photo of me—all in a single frame. The first three of these men were silk filature industrialists. Nino was not to follow suit. He decided to turn his life to a different kind of business than that of his forebears. He chose the export and import business between Italy and the U.S.; his wares included Italian culinary specialty items, from wine to chestnuts, and required frequent trips between Genoa and New York City.

Ercole Paredi, Bob's great-great-grandfather (1797-1861)

15

Giovanni Paredi, Bob's great-grandfather (1841-1916)

1. No-Man's Land, 1915-1918

Ercole Paredi, Bob's grandfather (1872-1960)

Giovanni "Nino" Paredi, Bob's father (1897-1980)

1. No-Man's Land, 1915-1918

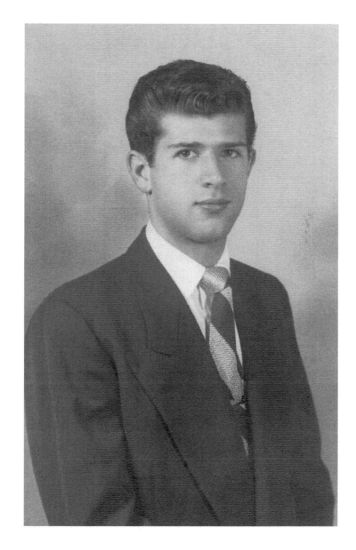

Robert "Bob" Paredi (1932-)

The American Legacy of an Italian Motorcyclist

2. The Immigrants

In the early 1900s, a recently married Italian couple, the Espostis, from the rural area surrounding Bologna, the culinary capital of Italy, was looking for greener pastures. They chose the Alsace-Loraine region of eastern France on the west bank of the upper Rhine River near Germany and Switzerland. The Espostis were part of a major exodus of economically depressed and poorly educated Italians motivated to improve their livelihoods. The Alsace-Lorraine area was known at the time as a hub of industrial development based on coal and iron mining and the steel industry. Such heavy industries relied upon the availability of large numbers of low-wage earners performing heavy labor around the clock.

Primo Esposti and his wife, Asunta, were the perfect couple to secure work as a steady and strong manager and cook-housekeeper for a "pensione"—a small boardinghouse for Italian laborers in the local mines and factories. About a dozen such laborers were boarding in the dwelling that the Espostis were placed in charge of managing. A few years passed, with Asunta doing all the cooking and housekeeping and Primo, his name indicating that he was the first offspring of his parents, doing the "managing."

One morning early in 1906, Asunta went to the office that was Primo's domain. He was nowhere to be found. But she noticed that the little safe was open and devoid of all the lodgers' earnings and minor valuables that they had entrusted Primo, not the local banks, to secure. A search of the neighborhood led to nothing. Primo had disappeared, leaving no note or other evidence of his whereabouts or destination. Consternation reigned; the lodgers had to keep working but volunteered to help Asunta in continuing to run the place. All were aware that Asunta was expecting her first child, who was soon born there, her daughter named Eda, on August 31, 1906.

Sometime after Eda's birth a telegram and money-order addressed to Asunta from Primo arrived, which instructed her to repay the lodgers for his "borrowings" and prepare to join him in San Francisco, California. She was also directed to invite one of the lodgers who was known to them and trusted by all, Gianni Dametti, to accompany mother and infant. The tickets were obtained and the threesome proceeded via New York City's Ellis

2. The Immigrants

Island Immigration Station to San Francisco by rail. Gianni accompanied Asunta and Eda all the way to San Francisco. They arrived in San Francisco months after April 18, 1906, the date marking the five-day catastrophe of the San Francisco earthquake and fire that practically destroyed the entire city. It was of 7.9 magnitude, killed as many as 3000 people, and obliterated eighty percent of the city. Relief supplies and funds arrived from all over the world, including quantities of raw lumber, which was immediately employed to construct hundreds of small cottages that displaced San Franciscans could rent for $5 a day until they were able to move to rebuilt or permanent dwellings.

Since Eda was born in Alsace-Lorraine at the end of August that year and arrived in San Francisco probably at least a month or two later, she, Asunta, and Gianni certainly got there as the city was hurriedly being reconstructed. The precise date of Primo's arrival there is unknown, but could have been shortly before or after the catastrophe of April 18, 1906.

The North Beach area of San Francisco was initially a well-defined Italian neighborhood. Other sectors of the city became known as Chinese or other ethnic neighborhoods. Gianni Dametti, who eventually became my godfather, soon found lodging and a career as a cook in a North Beach cafe. He retired back to Italy in 1950 with U.S.

23

Social Security benefits, never having had to learn a word of English. Primo eventually became a minor figure known to the police department and a few officers in the city administration. By the time that prohibition became the law of the land on Jan. 16, 1920, Primo had already developed his skills as a bootlegger. The illicit booze market greatly benefited as a result of prohibition, woman's suffrage, "flappers," jazz, and speakeasies.

Several banks had been established before the gold rush, including one small but popular bank within the Italian community called The Bank of Italy. Amadeo Peter Giannini, the first American-born son of an Italian immigrant, founded The Bank of Italy. All manner of people had profited from the well-publicized 1849 California gold rush, few of them literally striking gold to become rich. San Francisco's established merchants and some of the earlier immigrants certainly exploited the dramatically increased population spurred by the gold rush. Many prospered in the services sector, selling food, tools, clothing, entertainment, and liquor to the gold miners. Only a minority of the adventurers actually found enough gold to "strike it rich" by mining. However, Giannini's little Bank of Italy recovered from the 1906 earthquake and fire in rapid fashion as the result of his heroic efforts: using a horse-drawn cart, he personally rescued his bank's records, cash, and documents that had miraculously escaped the fire. His bank was the first in the city to open back up for business. Business boomed, and he eventually renamed his bank the Bank of America, which became the largest bank in the United States and possibly the world. That's what you call "striking it rich."

Prohibition was repealed on December 5, 1933, by the 21st Amendment, which repealed the 18th Amendment of January 16, 1919. However, Black Thursday had already launched the Great Depression with the stock market crash on October 24, 1929. Such was Primo's luck and reward that before the Great Depression he was financially successful enough to have built a beautiful three-story home on the ridge of one of the hills of San Francisco with a view of the Pacific Ocean and beaches. The home had two dining rooms, one of which could seat as many as 20 guests, often consisting of Primo's influential friends, city officials, and police. At such events Primo and Asunta's daughters—Eda, Erma, and Olga—were Asunta's kitchen aides and waitresses. The downstairs included a very large recreation room, complete with a ping-pong table and a player-piano with cabinets full of piano rolls. There, Eda and Erma would impress guests with their piano and violin performances. The basement consisted of a two-car garage and a secured large cold room containing about 20 large wooden barrels—barrels that were *not* used for water storage.

Eda and Erma, by the time they were 21 and 18 years old, had become well-educated and cultured young women. At 12, Olga was the youngest, and still in junior high. Eda and Erma attended a well-known vocational college for women in San Francisco, LUX College. Eda became a talented milliner, designing and constructing women's hats; Erma studied and practiced secretarial skills: typing, and shorthand. Eda and Erma also received private tutoring on piano and violin. In early 1927 Primo decided it was time for a family break involving a lengthy three-month trip to Italy for the entire family. A travel agent arranged their itinerary: train transport from Oakland across the bay, from San Francisco to New York City, three days of sightseeing in New York City, and lodging in the Knickerbocker Hotel. Substantial time in Italy was scheduled around the Bologna area for Primo and Asunta to show off their musically accomplished, bilingual daughters to their families.

Eda and Erma were both particularly pleased and motivated to travel and meet new people not necessarily acquainted with Primo's vocation and source of wealth. The daughters had been shamed often back in San Francisco while growing up in their first home, a rental. The cause of their embarrassment occurred one afternoon while returning from their local middle school. They arrived home to witness federal "revenue agents," as they were called during Prohibition, taking axes to demolish barrels of Primo's produce. It flowed for an hour down the gutters of the neighborhood. One can imagine the taunts and ridicule to which they were subjected at their young ages by their neighbors and schoolmates.

The SS *Roma*

The Espostis' departure for their Italian adventure was launched at a going-away party hosted by friends, their families, and the boyfriends of Eda and Erma. The most significant gift was a beautiful little leather-bound diary with a mechanical pencil, given to Eda by friends. Eda's family had forgotten about the diary by the time they boarded the steamship *Roma* on March 12, 1927. The diary was to get a workout by Eda on the voyage, but remained a secret until her death. The Espostis boarded the SS *Roma* in New York City to depart for Genoa, Italy, on March 12, 1927.

3. Eda's Secret Diary

Nino spent the years between 1918, his discharge from the Italian Army, and 1929 by launching an import-export business between Italy and the U.S. The trade started with chestnuts exported to New York City for the winter sidewalk vendors trade. Those years marked portentous political and economic developments in western Europe. At a personal level, Nino and his prosperous family witnessed the birth and rise of Umberto Mussolini's Socialist party, with its black-shirted acolytes staging demonstrations—and worse—all over Italy, particularly in Bologna. Commercial trade between Italy and the U.S. was starting to weaken, affecting his family's and Nino's own start-up business.

Nino happened to be concluding a business trip in New York City and was scheduled to return to Italy on the SS *Roma* on March 12, 1927. He and a business associate boarded the ship as planned.

They were used to such trips and not surprised by the rough waters for five days while traversing the Gulf Stream.

However, its effect on the occasional travelers on board was not so benign. Eda's entries in her secret diary were terse: 5 days from March 14 to March 18, only "Water, Water, Water, Water, Water." This period definitely dampened social activities aboard the SS *Roma*. But on its passing the diary revealed that Eda and Erma promptly became the "belles of the ball, the pretty flappers" of the SS *Roma*.

SS *Roma* bronze plaque souvenir

3. Eda's Secret Diary

Eda's secret diary entry on March 21 indicated a subtle but sudden change in her morale. During the shoreside excursion in Naples, the first stop of the SS *Roma*, she noted in her diary: "Naples obvious poverty depressed me. I was very glad that I was with a boyfriend I met on the ship who knew something about the city. I was very glad to get back to the ship. Sat out on the deck and watched the moon coming out in back of Mt. Vesuvius, it was a gorgeous sight. I will never forget it. Went to bed at 2 AM." This was the first use of the word "boyfriend"in her diary.

On March 22 the SS *Roma* finally docked in Genoa, marking the end of the sea voyage and starting the Esposti family's almost three-month tour of Italy, from the heel to the hip of the peninsula. They visited countless museums, monuments, and villas. Eda made no immediate mention of the "boyfriend" in the diary—he had left them to continue with his business dealings elsewhere in Italy.

The family went on an extensive tour of cities: Torino, Cuneo, Milano, and Bologna for a whole week of introductions to previously unknown relatives of the girls. There were grandparents, uncles and aunts, and cousins galore. Eda's diary entries range from very positive rankings of hotels they frequented to complaints: "Believe me, I met so many parents that I don't know yet who is who. Had plenty to eat and more to drink. Came back to

31

the hotel very tired." After another visit with new family members she enters in the diary: "Very sick and tired of eating and drinking so much. Very bad headache. Received a letter today."

The mention of this "letter" was the first cryptic clue of what was soon to follow. Eda's daily routine during this period in Bologna included guided visits, tours to historic sites, and daily banquets with normally distant but now becoming tiresome relatives. The Espostis were regularly feted by their families at the normal Italian midday suppers of exquisitely prepared Bolognese cuisine and wine. An additional challenge to the visitors was the saying and belief in Italy that "A la tavola non se invechia," meaning that "At the table one does not grow old." Therefore, the visitors were obliged to show their appreciation for the fine food and discourse, relax and enjoy.

Every few days during this period the diary has an upbeat entry such as "received a letter today" and "mailed a letter today" without mentioning the correspondent's name. On April 10th Eda and her family proceeded from Bologna to Florence for a few days of touring and sightseeing, then they went on to Rome, Naples, and the Lake Country of northern Italy and the little city of Como, site of the famously beautiful Lake Como. The traveling was always by arduous train journeys and long automobile rides between destinations, but the family was well attended by guides.

3. Eda's Secret Diary

Notably, Eda's diary has an entry on April 23: "In the beautiful little City of Como I received some letters today from Nino." Finally, the diary discloses the author's name, Nino, and we discover the connection the two have been developing over the weeks, facilitated by Eda's sharing of the family itinerary prepared by the travel agent. Nino knew very well the locations visited and hotels that harbored the Esposti family and probably how Eda felt about their growing relationship. From April 23, Eda and family proceeded to make their way back to Bologna via Pisa, Arona, Stresa, Lake Garda, Riva, Desanzano, and Venice, returning to Bologna on May 12.

At the end of the Venice visit Eda's diary entry refers to an exchange of gifts between Primo and Asunta on Asunta's birthday: "Found my mother with a wonderful pair of diamond earrings from Dad as a gift on her birthday. We also bought her a little gift. She is very happy. Well, I'm the only one that hasn't any rings now; it wouldn't make me sore if somebody got generous with me, however I'm not so crazy about them. Very tired out tonight, will now say goodnight to my dear little diary."

The family reunions resumed on May 13, with the tempo of letters increasing from Nino. Eda's diary continues: May 14: "Passed a very quiet & restful day. Had supper at my uncle's house saw my dear grandmother again. Received a letter also!" May 15: "Wrote a letter to my love this morning. Received another letter late tonight." May 16: "Shopping today, fixed myself a hat, received a postcard from San Remo where Nino was yesterday. Haven't answered his letter yet, bet he will have a fit. Walked around the city, very calm night." May 17: "Received another letter and postcard this morning. When I woke up it was underneath my door. Also answered it this morning." May 20: "Had a good time, got back at 3 AM. Feeling swell today, headache, feet hurt, sleepy, etc., etc. P.S. Received a letter also last night when I got there. Answered it this morning, made me very happy. Mother & Dad left this morning for Montecatini health resort so we kids are at the hotel all alone. This afternoon I'm going to a seamstress where I will start my suit. It's all cut and ready for the fitting. Made one of my house dresses, nearly completed. Very tired tonight."

To put Eda's quotidian diary musings in some historical context, the previous day's entry of May 20, 1927, marked the history-making trans-Atlantic, nonstop solo flight of Charles Lindbergh's landing in Paris from Roosevelt Field in New York in less than 34 hours. There was no mention of the event in her diary. Whether she was aware of it, or not, we may forgive her; sudden momentous events were about to occur in her own life. The diary between May 20 and May 26, 1927, mentions no letters arriving from Nino.

3. Eda's Secret Diary

But Eda kept busy designing a new wardrobe, reading a San Francisco newspaper, and visiting friends. Her diary resumes on May 28, 1927: "Feeling like hell today. Didn't get a letter yet from Nino so I decided to write a nice one to him myself. Got a letter from my Mother who is still in Montecatini. Going to get my new suit. Towards evening received a telegram! Very happy because my boyfriend will be with me tomorrow. Very happy tonight; going to get my new suit from the dressmaker." May 30, 1929: "Woke up early this morning, didn't sleep much. Went to see the King of Italy, very serious looking. Big doings in the city today, the 'Infante of Spain' is coming today, the football game between Italy & Spain is today. Went to the station to meet Nino but it was a cinch I would never find him in that crowd. Waited quite a while, finally someone patted me on the arm and I turned around and there he was. Gee, but I was glad. Spent the day talking things over. Went to three cafes. It sure is a relief to *conclude something.* Expecting the folks from Montecatini tomorrow." May 31, 1929: Bologna "Folks now with us, rushing all over the—."

That's it! Not another word. Eda's "dear little diary," which she started posting on March 14, 1927, abruptly and disappointingly simply stops: but *something* was *concluded.* No doubt, Primo, Asunta, Erma, and Olga were shocked. However, Eda no longer needed to seek solace and support

35

or an emotional outlet from her diary, as guardedly as she worded it. All those later diary entries about finely tailored new outfits were about her trousseau. What a read it would have been had she continued her diary! Eda's life immediately became dedicated to and filled with love for her Nino.

Many years later I discovered my mother's secret diary in her bedroom, when my wife, Sandra, and I were helping to prepare her Monterey, California, home to be sold.

The entire Esposti family, with Nino, traveled to Boves to meet Nino's family: father and mother—Ercole and Lucia—and his younger sisters—Franca and Maria—and young brother—Tomaso, called "Maso." The Esposti family was shown around the town and visited the silk filature factory and the convent, where Eda would be quartered for a month and regularly visited by Nino's sister, Maria.

According to Catholic Church custom, "bans" were posted for 30 days on the neighboring church doors announcing the wedding ceremony, and there was no way Eda could be housed at Nino's family residence during that period or be visited by Nino.

Eda's family was absent from Eda and Nino's wedding ceremony. This mystified me for a long time, since Eda's parents and sisters all returned to San Francisco prior to the ceremony. Many years later, the explanation for Eda's family's prompt departure prior to her wedding was still bothering me. My Aunt Erma finally explained the simple rationale. According to Aunt Erma, "Primo ran out of money and had to get back to business in San Francisco." It was that simple. The trip was over; the itinerary had been followed; the tour's budget was spent; the family was exhausted. It was time to return home to San Francisco.

Postcard of Boves, late 1920s; note the horse trough center left and the three school girls to the left

My parents' wedding took place on June 23, 1927, in the village of Marzaboto, Cuneo District of Piedmonte, officiated by Podesta Cavagliere Daniele Quadri and was formalized with signatures using a gold-quilled pen. Nobody from my mother's family or her San Francisco friends attended the wedding. The diary, pen, my father's medals, their wedding photos, and other memorabilia are held by me, their only child.

Eda Paredi, age 21, wedding photo

4. The New Families

Following Eda and Nino's wedding and honeymoon, Eda immediately became an integral part of the expanded Paredi family. The newlyweds settled in Nino's bedroom in the family home in Boves. Eda was not only quickly accepted but was well regarded since she was beautiful, bilingual, educated, and well-spoken in Italian. Nino's sisters, Maria and Franca, and his mother, Lucia, became intimate "stand-ins" for Eda's sisters and mother back home in San Francisco. Eda did not particularly miss her father, Primo. But her father-in-law, Ercole, was very impressed by her and must have welcomed the fact that she was an American citizen.

Nino kept busy trying to grow his import-export venture. However, the Italian business sector was showing signs of weakening, particularly in the international trade area. The Italian dictator-to-be, Benito Mussolini, was fomenting popular demonstrations feeding upon the poor economic growth of Italy's economy in the post-World War I era. The rapidly growing Fascist movement was especially distressing to the upper classes, and both Ercole and Nino saw the handwriting on the wall. Another war was developing as a result of Germany's situation and Mussolini's dream of forming Italian colonies in North Africa. Nino was reluctant to leave his family, but Ercole did not need to remind Nino how lucky he had been in avoiding the trenches due to Ercole's influence. He no doubt advised Nino to get out while the getting was good, and Nino just happened to have an American wife. Maria's and Franca's university educations would soon lead to their university professorships: Maria's in French history and language at the University of Turin, and Franca's in higher mathematics at the University of Milan. Nino's brother, Maso, would become a physician, but unfortunately would be drafted into the Italian Army and dispatched to Ethiopia in northeast Africa.

Two years after their June 1927 wedding, Eda and Nino, with mixed emotions, packed up and headed for San Francisco. Eda was homesick and a naturalized American citizen and Nino added to the influx of other foreign immigrants who feared what was developing in Europe: good news for those who had the initiative and means to leave, but bad news for Nino and Eda's immediate economic

4. The New Families

future. The U.S. economy crashed on "Black Thursday," which ushered in the Great Depression on October 24, 1929.

Eda was thrilled to return to San Francisco and be near her mother, Asunta, and her sisters, Erma and Olga—her Esposti family—in spite of her stressed relationship with her father, Primo. She quickly found employment at The City of Paris department store as a milliner. Primo had continued his bootlegging business, which relied on special treatment from certain politicians and the police department, and he continued to invite his supporters regularly to Asunta's fine Italian banquets in their spacious, newly built residence.

Primo welcomed his eldest daughter, Eda, and son-in-law, Nino. In fact, Primo was so pleased to welcome Nino that he offered him a job delivering Primo's products to his San Francisco clients. He hoped to extend the business far and wide into California with Nino's help. However, despite the Great Depression's effect on general employment, Nino rejected the offer, having been informed previously by Eda of Primo's character and social standing in the community. In doing so, Nino understandably put his job-searching at the mercy of luck and fortitude.

Prohibition was still in full swing, not to be repealed until 1933; the market for bootleggers' output continued to grow until then. Nino was of a prosperous and well-educated, law-abiding family. His decision to reject Primo's job offer was supported completely by Eda. Unfortunately, it resulted in a total breakdown of normal relations between the Esposti and Paredi families. Primo took Nino's rejection of his job offer personally, and the situation slowly led to much unhappiness between Primo and his wife and daughters. Having arrived in America, in spite of the non-existent job market, Nino felt secure in believing he had at least escaped from a deteriorating political and the increasingly militaristic and fascist environment in Italy. While Eda probably made enough money at The City of Paris department store's millinery department to put food on the table, Nino tried everything from chauffeuring, unloading rail cars, working in a goldmine, buying a gas station—finally settling on managing an apartment house in downtown San Francisco.

5. Erma's Idea

Upon the return of the members of the four Espostis to San Francisco in 1927, the two daughters, Erma and Olga, continued to be treated primarily as Asunta's helpers in carrying out her household and kitchen chores. Eda was surely missed, but was not part of Primo's family anymore. By 1930 Erma had concluded her education in the business and secretarial field. She decided to go it alone and moved out and easily found a job. Her education and statuesque beauty led to early success in the secretarial field. She enjoyed her independence and the escape from the drudgery and social ostracism of being known as a bootlegger's daughter.

One of her first employers was headed by a gentleman in San Francisco, Harold Stubley, definitely with a waspish moniker. He was a bit older than Erma and turned out to be an alcoholic. The marriage did not last, but Erma's new maiden name did: Miss E. Adelle Stubley. Having finally removed herself from the obvious association with the Italian community, Erma married again to a man with no Italian name but had no children. In her secretarial position she encountered gentlemen in various professions, including lawyers. She asked them for advice in the divorce field and soon became conversant in how such things are arranged and was somewhat familiar on the topic resulting from her failed marriage. She took the initiative to privately raise the topic with Asunta and Olga due to the deteriorating relationships between Asunta, Olga, and Primo.

Sure enough, the idea took hold: the divorce was settled, with Primo taking himself and his business to Oakland across the bay and leaving the lovely home to Asunta and her family. A few years after the divorce Asunta was introduced to a Spanish Catalonian gentleman who had escaped to San Francisco after eluding General Franco and his murderous dictatorial regime. Genis Mayolas considered himself lucky to have done so even though he had been a successful fabric designer and was giving up a decent profession. Once again, an immigrant arriving during the Great Depression did what he had to and Genis got a steady job as a janitor in a downtown Bank of America branch.

Asunta was introduced to Genis by his sister, Frances, who was a member of Asunta's local Catholic Church. In 1939 Asunta and Genis married, and he moved in with Asunta and was loved by everyone and admired for his hobbies—collecting elephant figures of all sizes and stamp collecting—and his carpentry skills. After WWII he bought a vacant lot above the banks of the Russian River, 60 miles north of San Francisco, where he personally designed and constructed a charming cottage that all the family enjoyed, including me during my summer school breaks, fishing and canoeing in the river. Even Erma supported the marriage, especially so since "Mayolas" did not sound like an Italian name.

Asunta and Genis

The American Legacy of an Italian Motorcyclist

I think that the American age of women's suffrage issues, such as employment, the vote, rampant male domination of accepted social and workplace behavior was receding around the time that Eda and Erma were maturing. Primo's autocratic expectations of how his older daughters would be expected to behave in Europe, from which they had luckily escaped, did not match Eda's nor Erma's expectations of acceptable practices now that they were Americans. Primo was a misogynistic tyrant as his two older daughters regarded him, because accepted normal behavior in Europe was not acceptable in America. Eda had escaped Primo's domestic tyranny by marrying an Italian who was soon to become an American citizen. Erma Adelle escaped Primo's behavior and expectations by developing a secretarial occupation and marrying her Mr. Stubley. These two young ladies convinced Asunta that her life would also be liberated to a better future by a divorce. Asunta, nonetheless, must have been a very courageous lady to go through with her divorce, but she had already shown her courage when, after having been pregnant and seemingly abandoned in Alsace-Lorraine 25 years earlier, she had traveled to the New World.

My earliest exposure to Asunta occurred after her divorce from Primo but before she met and married Mr. Genis Mayolas, the Spanish-Catalan. Many years later Nonna did have granddaughters, but I

5. Erma's Idea

was her first grandchild and the apple of her eye. She took every opportunity to take care of me when offered; even before I started school I was often consigned to Nonna's care, sometimes for days.

Asunta was an extremely happy lady. She would sing as she prepared her wonderful Bolognese cuisine and cuddled me during my pre-school years and loved to have me help in her kitchen chores. I now realize how she took advantage of her newfound freedom and was enjoying her new independence. And she continued to do so even after she shed Primo and remarried Genis, who bore no resemblance to Primo in any way.

My visits with my grandmother were welcome times for me. I would be expected to have afternoon naps for less than an hour on a special day-bed in Nonna's bedroom and then help her in the kitchen, which was her gifted avocation. I would follow her around the kitchen looking for an opportunity to help.

My first recollection of that help didn't turn out well, since Nonna had just withdrawn a pie from an oven and placed it high on a table. It looked and smelled so good that I reached high up and placed my hand right on the pie. For some reason the cure for burns in those days was to apply butter or olive oil to the burn instead of an ice cube. I realized many years later that refrigerators then did not produce ice cubes. Nonna felt so terrible about what she believed was her fault, but it was a lesson I never forgot.

As I got a bit older Nonna let me help her with the fun stuff. Much of her cooking time was spent at a big pasta-making table with a very smooth wooden surface. When the task was to make a quantity of ravioli, I always looked forward to operating the small steel-handled tool with a little steel wheel with a serrated circumference attached to its tip. On these occasions, Nonna would prepare two large sheets of pasta dough and a batch of cooked ground meat and sauce, the ravioli's stuffing. She would roll out two separate sheets of pasta, about 1/8-inch thick. Then she would evenly spread a batch of the stuffing meat with seasoning all over one of the sheets. The next step required her to carefully lay the second rolled-out pasta sheet over the sheet covered with the filling. Taking a large rolling-pin with square hollowed spaces all around its surface the size of a raviolo, she would place it at the edge of the two pasta sheets. Almost finished, she would run the rolling-pin forcefully from one end to the other over the two stuffing-filled sheets. This operation would not cut the sheets but press them together into a whole sheet of connected ravioli.

The fun part for me was to separate the pressed edges of ravioli into individual jagged-edged ravioli. All I had to do was carefully run the little steel-handled roller, in one direction at a time, along the

5. Erma's Idea

pressed-together lines of the two pasta sheets, then—presto!—scores of individual ravioli were finally produced, and I could then proudly announce to the gathered banquet guests that I had made the ravioli. I still have that little steel roller to this day in a kitchen drawer.

Nonna's ravioli tool

Another culinary lesson I learned from Nonna was how to make "gnocchi" (pronounced nee-AWK-eee). Gnocchi are unique because they are essentially little potato dumplings made of potatoes and eggs instead of wheat flour and eggs. Once I learned how they were made, they were arguably much easier to make than ravioli. However, Nonna did use plenty of "elbow grease" in the process of making the potato dough. After boiling the peeled white potatoes she would mash them to a very fine puree-like consistency. Then she would heap it all into a pile, drive her fist into the center of the potato puree and break several whole eggs into that depression and start manually kneading the pile of the potatoes and eggs into a homogeneous mass that would not slump, adding another egg if it did.

When a double handful of the dough could be separated from the mass she would hand-roll it into a random length of roughly uniform circumference about three-quarters of an inch in diameter. Nonna would then cut cylinders off of the dough-roll about 1-1/2 inches long. She would continue producing the little cylindrical potato dumplings from the remaining dough. If the dough got too tacky to handle, she would sprinkle a bit of flour on the table and on the long rolls of dough. She would have a large pot of salted water boiling by this time.

5. Erma's Idea

This is when the fun began for me. Nonna taught me to hold a four-tined table fork motionless upside-down, with my left hand holding the fork at a 45-degree angle to the top of the table with all of the fork's tines pressed against the table. I would pick a single dumpling at a time, thumb under the cylinder and index and middle finger on the top of the cylinder. With moderate pressure in a continuous motion I would then roll the single dumpling at an angle across the fork's stationary tines with a quick flip of the wrist. It took me dozens of times to get it right. I finally mastered the trick and learned to go quickly through the whole pile to get each little dumpling to have a hollowed-out interior and a four-ridged exterior. They were no longer cylinders, and they were then ready to dump all together into the pot of boiling water. The gnocchi would all sink to the bottom of the pot and very soon rise to the boiling water's surface properly cooked. Nonna would immediately scoop them all up and place them in a large serving bowl containing the sauce she would have prepared ahead of time.

So, what's the big deal about creating hollowed-out little dumplings with three or four little ridges on each of their backs? Not hollowed out with no ridges, they just drown in the sauce, not holding it. Before ordering gnocchi in any Italian restaurant, ask to see one before they are cooked: not hollowed or ridged, don't order them!

The American Legacy of an Italian Motorcyclist

Starting in 1938, the social relationship between the Paredi and Mayolas families launched many years of normal loving relations, birthday celebrations, and holiday banquets. It was during this period that I was included in the frequent family banquets involving the members of the Mayolas and Paredi families, and their many friends and guests.

Christmas celebrations were major family affairs at Nonna and Genis' home. For the first time I saw an electric train set around the base of a Christmas tree and I was mesmerized by it. And every Christmas thereafter the train set got more and more extensive and complicated. Genis had a similar child-like fascination with the idea. Villages, tunnels, stations, and animal statues small and large were added from year to year, particularly from his constantly growing elephant collection, which eventually reached into the hundreds of pieces. One never had to wonder what to get Genis for his birthday or other event. His collection grew steadily.

We always had a tree at our home, but the Christmas tree at Nonna's home on a far wall next to a huge roaring fireplace was a spectacle that the whole family looked forward to and always brought a new ornament to add to the display. And Nonna's Christmas meal in the adjacent large dining room, which all of her daughters had helped with from

5. Erma's Idea

early in the day, did justice to the Italian belief that "a la tavola non se invecchia."

The only mechanical or electrical communication devices found in homes back then were the telephone and radio: there were no televisions, no computers, no cell phones. Children were to be "seen and not heard"; they might be seated together at the same table with adults but were expected to behave themselves and do no more than respectfully listen to the opinions, arguments, and jokes of the adults. All of the frequent family banquet guests were bilingual, with some combination of English with Italian, French, and Spanish, depending on the guest's nationality. English however was not the preferred language of choice among some of the recent immigrants. The children might be addressed in English, but the foreign languages often prevailed and to the children seemed to be "going in one ear and out the other." It seemed so to the kids at the time, but did it?

Several years later, when I was 16 years old, I had to spend more than three months with my mother, my Italian aunt Maria; her young son, Sandro; and my father's mother, my paternal grandmother, Lucia, in Turin, Italy. I had studied French in high school for four years by then, but my mother and Maria, a professor of French language and history, only had the Italian language in common. So, Italian was the language spoken in Maria's apartment during the months we all spent together. All those years that I had spent as a kid being seen and not heard, and not growing old...the Italian language wasn't just going in one ear and out the other. Some of it got stuck in my brain and came out through my vocal chords in the several weeks that we all lived with Maria in 1949.

6. Making a Living

Unsurprisingly, my father found it a struggle to find decent employment in America under the conditions of the deep and persistent Great Depression, which lasted almost to the beginning of World War II. He started with part-time dock work unloading trains and cargo ships along the San Francisco waterfront. He even tried an underground gold mine in northern California. The wealthy Crocker banking family hired him as a chauffeur for a year or so. He eventually found steady employment as the manager of a small hotel in downtown San Francisco. That led to a similar position with a large apartment house on "Nob Hill," an upscale neighborhood within walking distance downhill to Market Street, the commercial center of the city. While dad had mastered the English language by then, he never lost his characteristic Italian accent.

The American Legacy of an Italian Motorcyclist

My mother, being a skilled milliner, found decent and secure employment in the women's hat department at The City of Paris department store near Market Street. San Francisco was widely known in those days as a city where every woman wore a hat to be considered properly attired, and those who could afford it had their hats designed and custom-made by mom, who designed and constructed hats in direct contact with customers of The City of Paris Hat Shop. Mom loved her work and only occasionally complained about her boss, Madam Olga!

Eda Paredi (on right) with Madam Olga

6. Making a Living

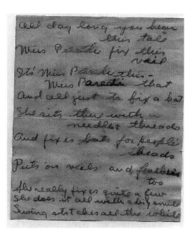

My mom's poem, scribbled on scrap paper

All day long you hear this tale:
Miss Paredi fix this veil.
It's Miss Paredi this, Miss Paredi that
And all just to fix a hat.
She sits there with a needle and threads
And fixes hats for people's heads
Puts on veils and feathers too
She really does quite a few
She does it all with a big smile
Sewing stitches all the while.

57

Postcard view of The City of Paris, circa the 1930s

After my birth in 1932, we lived in rented properties until the family's fortunes improved in the late 1930s. My mother quit work just long enough to care for me for several years, until I entered first grade in a public school a few blocks from the apartment house that my father managed, only two blocks from the center of "Chinatown." That apartment house, at 1020 Powell Street, is located on the most favored cable-car route of tourists visiting San Francisco. The cars traverse a fixed route between Market Street and San Francisco's Fisherman's Wharf, about a half-hour each way, with frequent stops for travelers to dismount and board. The cable cars are propelled by a constantly moving cable at a fixed speed below the street in a trench at the center of the cars' wheel tracks. Many tenants of private and public properties get used to the humming and clattering noise that the cable produces 24 hours per day.

San Francisco's famous cable cars

The grease that the miles-long cable is lubricated with has a peculiar odor that I can still recall, along with the persistent clattering sound of the cable. Each cable car carried about 60 passengers between its center enclosed section and its fore and aft open sections. At each end of the route a turntable is located to rotate the empty cable car 180 degrees to orient its course in the opposite direction. This operation seems to provide a favorite "photo-op" to crowds of tourists. The cable car's crew consists of the toll collector and the brakeman. The latter manages two long levers, the foot of each projecting through the center trench between the car's wheel-tracks to either grip the cable to pull the car up grades or to grip the underside of the cable trench housing to control the downhill speed of the car as the brake is applied. Mounted atop the roof of the car is a large brass bell whose clapper rope hangs down by the brakeman's side for him to yank while crossing intersections or to entertain tourists.

At full normal passenger capacity, additional passengers were allowed to stand under the roofs of the open sections and ride on the running boards while gripping stationary hold bars. There were occasional accidents involving automobiles and standing passengers, but the crews have little control over some particularly young and daring passengers. The cable cars loaded with passengers followed a route north to Fisherman's Wharf and back, through and over the same hills up and down the city to Market Street. It still is the original and ongoing commercial thoroughfare of "the city by the bay."

6. Making a Living

Several years ago there was a reduction in the number of cable-car routes traversing the town, but tourism-industry resistance prevented the total elimination of the popular and unique cable-car system.

A postcard view of Market Street, circa the 1930s

The American Legacy of an Italian Motorcyclist

My first exposure to little kids of my age was on Powell Street, when dad got his first full-time job as the manager of the four-story apartment house two blocks west of Grant Avenue, the main street of the mile-long heart of Chinatown. The next door up-hill establishment was the sidewalk display window and entrance to a furrier's shop operated by an immigrant Chinese gentleman with his wife and three children. Their ground floor apartment extended all the way back from the entrance to a large garden that extended up a steep slope behind the apartment building. My parents and I occupied an apartment on the second floor of the building, my dad being the "concierge" of the building of about 20 separate apartments. The four of us—me and the three Chinese children—were the only kids on the whole block. I started public school there a few blocks down the hill in the first grade—no kindergarten.

My first childhood memories were created at our apartment: my mom combing and tending my hair, completely blond then, four years old or so, and playing with the little Chinese kids, a boy and two girls, in the backyard. The kids were around my same age. There was no playing on the sidewalk or in the busy Powell Street of regular vehicle traffic and the cable cars. We four thought we were the only kids in the world. Outside of school days the Chinese kids' mother would sit the four of us down on the floor of their dining room, which had no "dining" table. While I don't remember what the menu was, I do recall its delicious sweet and sour aromas. I never did learn to use chopsticks properly, so I probably was presented with western tableware.

A very young Bob

I remember a minor accident I suffered one day when I was playing on the living room floor near a large flower pot. I slipped, fell forward, and cracked my head just below my hairline, which immediately started to bleed severely. I started to scream and cried; mom ran in to gather me up and chased down my father from somewhere in the building. They drove me just a few blocks to the Saint Francis Hospital on Nob Hill, where I had been born. I was sat down on the edge of a table while I watched the doctor pass a threaded needle through my scalp seven or eight times, not feeling a thing. I think my mom was more upset than I was because, while I never felt a thing, she had to watch the procedure. The cut left a little scar at my hairline above my right eye for several years before it disappeared.

The tenants of the apartment house on Nob Hill that my father managed then were an odd lot. Those were the ones who, for some reason, became my parents' good friends. One was Osborn Parker from Alabama, a middle-aged insurance salesman who had collected a huge number of old wax and Bakelite recordings of classical music featuring world-famous Italian opera singers. As a young man in Italy, my father had been an opera fan and was familiar with those artists. Osborn also hosted a regular Saturday morning local radio program featuring recordings from his collection, which dad really enjoyed. Dad often brought me along to Osborn's apartment to listen to the recordings that he had selected for an upcoming broadcast. I eventually suspected that my father had me

6. Making a Living

accompany him to Osborn's as a form of classical music appreciation. The records had to be treated carefully and Osborn never deployed steel needles upon them, which would inevitably subject the wax and Bakelite records to excessive wear.

I was made useful by being taught how to employ a little device to sharpen the bamboo "needles" after the records were played. Each "needle" was made from an inch-long slip of bamboo of triangular cross-section an eighth of an inch wide on each side. My job was to insert the bamboo slip in the device, which was fitted with a sharp razor blade at an angle with the bamboo slip. I would then give a whack to the handle of the blade-holder with the heel of my hand. This would shave a thin and worn slice of bamboo off of the bamboo slip at a fixed 45-degree angle to produce a needle-sharp point at its tip. The same bamboo needle could be used for several plays before becoming too short to sharpen in the device. To dad's and Osborn's credit was my early education in classical music and bamboo needle fabrication.

Two of the other tenants were Anton Cufari, a hair-dresser, and a glamorous and single Latina woman, Yolanda, of unknown employment. When the famous Mexican bandleader Xavier Cougat and his orchestra would be on a performance tour visiting the Golden Gate Theater on Market Street, dad would arrange to rent the apartment house's vacant rooms to the orchestra during its San

Francisco gig. We would attend a performance of Cougat's orchestra at the theater, where I was particularly impressed with the performance of Cougat's trumpeter.

I also saw the first two movies of my life at the Golden Gate Theater, *Fantasia* and *Pinocchio*. On the next corner, on Powell Street, up-hill from the apartment house, was a pharmacy/coffee and ice-cream parlor owned and operated by Hy Cohen, who also became a pal of my father's. Hy was Jewish and often teased my father of being a "closet Jew," due to dad's somewhat "Roman" nose. The pharmacy and its small soda fountain was kind of a gathering place in the neighborhood. "Banana splits" at the long counter cost around 50 cents, and a "coke" a nickel.

Hy and his wife had two young sons, Ivan and Carter, who were about six and eight years old at the time. Hy complained about Carter waking up in the small hours of the night, kneeling at the head of his bed in front of his pillow, and repeatedly banging his head against the wall. On the other side of the wall was his parents' bedroom and Hy would have to wake up Carter, who would return to sleep, sometimes repeating this performance more than once a night. Dad offered to cure Carter of the habit within a month. Because Hy was skeptical but desperate, I ended up with Carter as a roommate.

6. Making a Living

My father spent a day or two constructing a contraption to install over Carter's bed next to mine. Dad built a paddle resembling a flimsy leaf-rake to set up over Carter's bed. It was attached to a hinge high on the wall above Carter's head with a rope attached to the rake's shaft just above the rake-like end. The other end of the rope passed through a hole in the wall above Carter's bed, which adjoined my parents' bedroom. The rope's end hung down from the hole to a height within reach of dad's hand. Dad also attached a stick with three little bells to the wall near the rope's end; the bells would jingle as Carter was banging his head against the wall. When the bells rang, dad, half asleep and not rising, would pull on the rope to raise and lower the paddle a couple of strokes up and down to pat Carter's rump as he was banging his head against the wall. This would wake Carter up and he would return to sleep. After a few weeks of Carter's successful "treatment," my father returned Carter to his parents, who were as thrilled as I was, and dad became the hero of the drugstore/fountain crowd.

Carter's brother, Ivan, and I were buddies and would roughhouse together, so my father taught us to try and play nicely by teaching us fencing, which had been dad's favorite sport before going to war in Italy long before then. Dad also set us up once with a task that exhausted us in less than an hour. The apartment house furnished all of the apartments' kitchens with dinner plates, bowls, glasses, and so on. The slightest chip, or worse, on a piece required dad to replace the damaged articles. My father had quite a collection of the damaged items in boxes in the basement near the garbage chute, which fed into a huge collection bin, which was emptied weekly by the garbage collectors. Dad set me and Ivan up near the top of the bin close to the dozens of boxes full of damaged goods. He directed us to empty every box by crashing its contents to the bottom of the bin. It was noisy and wonderful fun for us for about 30 minutes, but then became tiring and boring and we were thankful to finish the job.

7. Growing Up

I skipped second grade for some reason and after I completed third grade we moved from Powell Street to the mostly Italian neighborhood of North Beach, 330 Lombard Street, on Telegraph Hill overlooking San Francisco Bay. There I was surrounded by Italian American families and kids, mostly boys my age. I missed my little Chinese neighbors, who were not that far away. But both our families probably needed to learn how to quickly adapt to new lives and surroundings, and my parents never offered me the opportunity to visit those kids and their mom. I wish they had, but I never asked.

Dad found a skilled-labor position as an electrician at Mare Island Naval Shipyard, north of the Golden Gate Bridge. It was one of 16 shipyards all across America that were involved in building over 2700 cargo-carrying "Liberty Ships," which were a part of the "Lend Lease Program" in the lead-up to and during WWII as part of America's effort to support England's defense against Germany.

In this North Beach neighborhood I made many new friends and attended Saints Peter and Paul Church with my mother, and its associated Salesian Boy School. The school's instructors, Salesian "brothers," were tough school teachers and in charge of my education for three years, from the third through fifth grade. I was also a member of the church boys choir, which often sang for special Masses behind the pipe-organ at the rear top loft of the famous church, at which years later Joe DiMaggio and Marilyn Monroe were wed. The entire church and school complex was only a 15-minute walk downhill from our home, which was five minutes downhill from Coit Tower, a landmark at the summit of Telegraph Hill.

Even though I never saw Joe DiMaggio play baseball, as a boy I was very familiar with his story, and followed his exploits for my entire life. "Joltin' Joe" DiMaggio was born in Martinez, across the bay from San Francisco on November 25, 1919, to an Italian immigrant family whose father was a commercial fisherman. At 19 years of age in his first full season with the Pacific Coast League San Francisco Seals, he hit safely in 61 straight games, a record which stood for 80 years. With the New York Yankees in 1941 he had a 56-game hitting streak and led the Yankees to nine championships in 13 years. His lifetime batting average was .325, with 361 home runs and 1,537 runs batted in. After serving three years with the U.S. Army in World War II, he returned in 1946 to lead the Yankees to another world championship, hitting .290 with one fielding error. After 13 years in the major leagues, he retired and eventually married Marilyn Monroe in 1954 at Sts. Peter and Paul Church, the same church I attended as a boy, adjacent to the Salesian Boy's School. That marriage lasted only nine months, but by the 1960s they were back together again, planning to remarry. After Marilyn's suicide in 1962, Joe claimed her body and arranged the funeral. Three times a week for 20 years he had roses sent to her crypt. After his death in 1999, it was said that his last words were "I finally get to see Marilyn."

I regularly attended Sunday Masses with my mother, Eda, a devout Catholic, and eventually undertook Holy Communion and Confirmation rituals with mother in attendance. After my Confirmation I found every excuse possible to avoid attending church with mom. My father was agnostic and held the Catholic Church and its priests in low esteem, and would even at times make rude jokes about them and their supposed tendency to abuse young boys. I was never aware of this issue at my young age, but dad probably would never have permitted me to become an altar boy. I never saw dad in any church with the exception of a wedding. However, my father

71

respected mom's commitment to the Catholic religion and her devotion to its church.

I don't remember going to public libraries in San Francisco. But my parents saw to it that a subscription to the "Encyclopedia Britannica" was purchased for my use throughout my school years. I recall that from the fourth grade until I graduated from high school I made regular use of it and its annual publication of an update volume. We also received home delivery of *Time, Life*, and *National Geographic* magazines, and I regularly read comic books like the *Lone Ranger, Superman, Spiderman*, and *Batman*.

There were a few years between my ages of eight and eleven more or less when I was broadly hinting that I was really wondering if I would be given a bike for Christmas. A lot of the other kids had bikes. I think that my mom always vetoed the idea. I never complained about it because I felt then that the budget was the issue. But I was an "only" child in a crowded town with growing traffic and suspect that my mom was the problem. Nonetheless, my dad felt that I had to learn how to operate a bike. When living on Telegraph Hill prior to WWII he must have gotten grudging approval from mom to take me to a flat bike instruction location down by the waterfront where kids would go with their dads to rent a bike and flounder around the flat, unpaved lot and learn the skill. I recall that after one summer of six or eight weekend days of dad's

7. Growing Up

help I figured it out and was a qualified cyclist without a bike.

One summer after moving away from Telegraph Hill I was demonstrating to some of my new friends that I was able to ride their bikes. Later on, one of them asked me to do him the favor of delivering newspapers for a week since his parents were to take him someplace and he did not want to lose his customers. I don't recall asking my parents for permission to do so, but I did it and had no problems. I wonder if dad knew what was going on and never made an issue of it with my mom. It certainly was a far less trafficked neighborhood than Telegraph Hill.

Having done without a piano for many years during their marriage, my mother always hoped that the day would come when they could afford a piano. That day came in 1943, when dad gave her the birthday gift of a brand-new piano in our Telegraph Hill top-floor apartment. Until then she only had the opportunity to play the piano at Asunta's home, after the fortuitous divorce of Asunta and Primo.

I am convinced that when my dad bought the piano it improved the quality of our lives. Frederick Chopin plus other classical composers' music suddenly appeared. Dad certainly appreciated Italian opera, but I don't recall ever hearing him whistle or humming a tune. When mom got her

73

musical "chops" back after dad got his breakthrough job with the U.S. Navy and the piano appeared, our home was, outside of working hours, filled with her enthusiastic but sensitive piano playing.

At the beginning of WWII my mother hoped to teach me to play the piano. I was "incentivized" to practice by mom dropping a dime into a little bank that rested atop the piano for every day that I practiced. I eventually managed to haltingly perform the Army Air Forces, Marine Corps, and the Navy anthems. However, first came the scales in the key of C with both hands. I could not ignore that my left-hand reach was a bit limited. I probably thought it would mean that I would never master the piano, no matter how hard I tried. The problem with the little finger on my left hand was that it was absent! It was missing because I was born without it. Mom did not make a big deal about it, but she surely knew why I gave up trying to master the instrument.

Even though mom tried everything to teach me to play the piano, dad, however, did get me interested in learning how to handle his large collection of hand tools, how to repair electrical devices, and a fascination with mechanical devices, an example of which was the early juke-box.

To mom's chagrin, sometime after she got her own piano, dad showed up one day with an odd-looking

74

tall wooden cabinet with glass windows on the front and the two sides, within which was a Ferris wheel-looking device with a dozen or so carriages, each of which loaded with a wax cylinder about 2-1/2 inches in diameter and six inches long.

These cylinders were the first records that Thomas Edison had invented upon which one might record sound, preferably music. Two crank handles protruding through the antique woodwork of the tall cabinet allowed the customer to rotate the "Ferris wheel" with a particular wax cylinder to the fixed position under the pickup mechanism. The customer would then employ the other external lever to lower the needle attached to its pickup device onto the surface of the wax cylinder, with its needle resting upon its first groove. Lastly, the customer had to load a nickel into a slot device and slide the coin into the internal collection container to unlock the contraption, rotate another wind-up crank to provide the power to rotate the cylinder beneath the needle, lean back and enjoy a maximum of three minutes of music. That was the first juke box!

My father had found the juke box in an old bar in North Beach, and bought it at a get-rid-of-it price with a collection of wax cylinder musical recordings to show it off to friends, relatives, and my pals. The three-minute finite capacity of a wax cylinder became the commercial standard for several generations for the maximum length for any kind of recordings in the industry. That standard remained so until 9- and 11-inch diameter long-playing vinyl discs were developed and introduced by the recording industry. Dad had a boundless interest in mechanical devices.

My father was not particularly interested in fishing, however, as I discovered many years later, even though he took me and Osborn Parker to one of the piers on the San Francisco Bay to fish during World War II. I was about 10 years old and fascinated with a contraption dad constructed to make the pastime more efficient and entertaining. At the end of every one of the huge piers was a large bulkhead constructed of railroad ties, which confined a railroad bumper to help exactly locate the string of freight cars opposite the warehouse sections on the pier. Dad designed and built a fishing trolley. We would drive to the bay waterfront, park the car, unload its components, and carry them to the end of the pier. We would then bolt the critical piece onto the inner surface of the four-foot-high timber bulkhead: the piece was a six-foot-long broom handle. On its top was a small pulley through which we would pass a long rope, the end of which was tied to an anchor heavy enough to pitch out into the bay. After letting the anchor sink to the water bottom, we would pull the anchor rope until the anchor set with a moderate pull. To eventually retrieve the anchor, we would simply apply more force to the rope and pull it in.

7. Growing Up

The shore-end of the anchor line was passed through the small pulley atop the broom handle and secured to a hook on the bottom of the broom handle. This rope would be the fixed line along which would ride a small conveyance suspended from two small pulleys riding along the secured anchor line from the top of the broom handle.

The two-foot-long conveyance, attached to a light line, was fitted with three fish-hooks loaded with bait and deployed to any desired depth. A small bell was attached to the pulley through which the running trolley line passed at the top of the broom handle. The ringing bell announced a fish was hooked! It was so much fun operating the rig it mattered not whether any fish were caught, but we often did bring fresh fish home for a fine Sunday wartime meal.

Other Sunday family pastimes were my pony rides and dad's interest in motorcycle races. After breakfast and church for mom and me, dad would often take us to the Twin Peaks area so I could ride one of the docile ponies at the nearby riding stable. This very large hill consists of two identical peaks and is a popular tourist location at the center of town, affording a 360-degree view of the five-mile by five-mile expanse of the hilly city, from the Pacific Ocean to the San Francisco Bay and beyond.

The American Legacy of an Italian Motorcyclist

The pony riding stable was at the foot of Twin Peaks. It was great fun to ride the pretty little ponies quietly around the track for a half hour or so. But the really exciting attraction was to go to a nearby smaller hill to watch young motorcyclists trying to avoid breaking their necks. The adjoining parking lot would be packed with cars of spectators who came to view the steep slope of the small hill with a 200-yard dirt track running straight up to the top of it at about a 45-degree angle.

The cyclists would take turns, one at a time, gunning their engines at the foot of the slope and taking off. These were time-trials to determine which rider could make it to the finish line at the top in the shortest time without capsizing or otherwise losing control of their "bikes." The crowd would cheer all riders who made it to the finish line at the top, or gasp as a rider might take a spectacular spill before crossing the line.

Every Sunday at least one of the 20-plus cyclists would suffer some kind of spill; we never saw any of them get killed, but did see some too injured or discouraged to have another go. Back home on Telegraph Hill, one day our landlady's young adult son, Nelson, a keen motorcyclist, was killed in a crash with an automobile. The accident occurred just a few blocks from home at an intersection that I crossed every day to and from school. I realized then that it would not be received well by my father, ever in the future, for me to mention wanting a motorcycle. Dad also never referred to Nelson's fatal accident. He also never had to warn me about the risks of operating a motorcycle. Nonetheless, dad really got a kick out of the motorcycle hill-climbing races we witnessed, while probably imagining how he might have handled that hill and the competition. No doubt he compared the smooth dirt track of that hill to the no-man's lands that he successfully maneuvered for four years on his Indian bike with its attached side-car. My father probably thanked his lucky stars and realized how fortunate he had been to survive his World War I experience. While watching those San Francisco hillside motorcycle races, I came to wonder if my father had ever felt that one day his luck would run out.

Telegraph Hill is the most dominant hill in North Beach, the Italian area of San Francisco, having an unobstructed view of the San Francisco Bay. The hill owes its name to the fact that in the city's early days a flag pole, and eventually a telegraph station, was located there. An attendant would signal to the relatively small Mexican settlement of the time when a sailing ship was observed entering the San Francisco Bay through the relatively narrow "Golden Gate," the northern extent of, and the only entrance to, the great bay.

Such an event was very important to the original San Francisco community. It signaled that commercial opportunities would soon arrive along the beaches, and eventually at a profusion of piers constructed along the northern beaches of the city's bayfront. All kinds of cargo—from raw materials to new settlers, animals, or equipment— were arriving from the eastern American industrial factories, Asia, and Mexico. All of this would lead to local employment, trade, and development. The ship would finally be identified as it approached the bay's beaches and be welcomed by city officials, traders, and laborers offering their services.

However, Telegraph Hill became much more of a landmark in 1933, with the completion at its summit of an Art Deco-styled, 210-foot-tall fluted concrete cylinder called Coit Tower. It is a stunning look-out post, art museum, and memorial dedicated to the American laborer, specifically firefighters. It also has become recognized as a nationally significant landmark and appears in the National Register of Historic Places. The tower's namesake, Lillie Hitchcock Coit, was an early San Francisco philanthropist and an "adorer of local firefighters." The role that firefighters played in saving San Francisco from the ravages of the widespread fires caused by the 1906 earthquake was fresh in the minds of its citizens 30 years later.

Lillie was quite flamboyant in her admiration of firefighters and was occasionally seen dressed as a firefighter. She was known to pursue manly pastimes, such as sharpshooting and gambling. Upon her death in 1929, $125,000 of her estate was given to San Francisco "to be expended in an appropriate manner for the purpose of adding to the beauty of the city which I have always loved."

My Telegraph Hill family home from 1937 to 1942, at 330 Lombard Street on the northern edge of a ridge, provided a spectacular view. My bedroom windows facing due north overlooked a 180-degree view of the bay from west to east. To the west was the Marina District and the Golden Gate Bridge, next was Alcatraz Island, then Treasure Island and the San Francisco-Oakland Bay Bridge. Every one of these structures, areas, and locations has its own story, significance, and value to California, to the rest of America, and to the world.

The Marina District was a relatively new San Francisco development owing to its precursor, the Panama Pacific International Exposition (PPIE), which opened in February 1915 and closed in December 1915. President Theodore Roosevelt conceived the PPIE as a worldwide celebration of the Panama Canal's opening. The PPIE was planned several years before the 10-year construction of the Panama Canal concluded. The Canal opened to maritime commercial traffic in August 1915. Long before then a 650-acre area on the northwest corner of San Francisco along the beachfront of the "Golden Gate" was selected for the PPIE construction. The area was lightly developed, strategically located, and accessible to transportation facilities necessary to deliver the massive amount of construction equipment and material required. From the time that ground clearing started until the three-year construction was concluded, 11 exhibition palaces, 21 foreign pavilions, 48 State buildings, and a 65-acre amusement zone were constructed, for a total of 200 buildings. A revolutionary decision by the architects and designers of the huge PPIE facility was to restrict the color palette of every structure's exterior to seven "natural colors": earth tones, vegetation's natural colors, soft pastels, rock, natural water's and minerals' colors—these colors all produced an aura of aged and classical beauty. The objective of the classical colors' motif was to remedy San Francisco's reputation as an uncouth frontier town with an anti-immigration sentiment. The PPIE's iconic structure, the "Tower of Jewels," at 432 feet high, was covered with thousands of multicolored bits of colored glass to impart a night-time shimmering display when illuminated with beams of special lighting projected from vessels in the bay.

The PPIE was also intended to demonstrate to the world that San Francisco had not only recovered from the 1906 catastrophic earthquake and fire in a mere nine years but the city was capable of mounting the most successful exposition ever,

7. Growing Up

which attracted almost 19 million visitors in 10 months and turned a profit of $1.3 million. Roosevelt's successful mission and that of his numerous supporters and visionaries more than satisfied their expectations. The PPIE did have an incalculably positive effect upon many nations at a time when WWI was just exploding.

Postcard from the Panama-Pacific Exposition, 1915

The American Legacy of an Italian Motorcyclist

The next view in the panorama that my bedroom window presented to me every morning while preparing to walk to school was the Golden Gate Bridge. It led from the vicinity of the PPIE site, whose entire infrastructure, save three buildings, including the Palace of Fine Arts, had been quickly demolished to make way for the development of the San Francisco Marina District. The Golden Gate Bridge, completed in 1933, connected the Presidio District in San Francisco to Marin County directly across the Golden Gate Strait of the Pacific Ocean leading into San Francisco Bay.

"The Most Photographed Bridge in the World"

7. Growing Up

The main hazard facing the bridge's construction crews was the 300-foot water depth that the two tower's foundations had to be built in; deep-sea divers were among the 10 worker fatalities. Repetitive fogs also caused delays and contributed to accidents. Nonetheless, the Golden Gate Bridge's fame is such that it is considered to be the most photographed bridge in the world, and serves as a convenient access to Sausalito in Marin County and the northern California coast.

Almost due north from my bedroom window was Alcatraz Island, occupied entirely by the infamous high security federal prison. The island covers 22 acres and lies 1.5 miles north of the Marina District on a rocky island, referred to as "the Rock" by its inmates. "Alcatraz" is the Spanish word for pelican. It was first explored by the Spanish in 1775 and sold to the U.S. in 1849. Alcatraz became the site of the first lighthouse on the California coast in 1854. Its early buildings served to house an Army detachment. Then in 1861 it started serving as a prison for military offenders and some Hopi Indians from the Arizona Territory. It also held American soldiers who deserted and joined the Philippine cause for independence in 1900.

The American Legacy of an Italian Motorcyclist

1936 postcard view of Coit Tower and Alcatraz

In 1907 Alcatraz became part of the U.S. Military Prison System. Between 1934 and 1963 it housed the most dangerous of civilian prisoners, including Al Capone, George ("Machine Gun") Kelly, and Robert Stroud, the "Birdman of Alcatraz." In 1963 the prison was closed down due to excessive operating costs. After several years of occupation by Native American groups claiming sovereign rights to the island, the National Park Service made a wide area of the island accessible to the public to enjoy its scenery and bird, marine, and animal life.

The San Francisco Oakland Bay Bridge, at the eastward limit of my bedroom panorama, traverses

7. Growing Up

a tunnel passing through Yerba Buena Island connecting to the second half of the bridge to Oakland. The San Francisco half has two suspension spans and the remainder from Yerba Buena Island to Oakland is of conventional truss design. Both sections have an upper and lower deck, the latter having half for railroad and half for vehicular traffic. Considerable redesign and reconstruction of the Oakland final sections of the bridge became necessary due to the Loma Prieta earthquake in October 1989. Rail traffic has been supplanted by passenger bus service and one-way traffic on each deck of the bridge. The advent of the two bridges, the Golden Gate and the San Francisco Bay, has essentially replaced the large fleet of ferries that once served as the only transportation available between the San Francisco Peninsula and the Marin County and East Bay communities.

Yerba Buena Island (Spanish for "good grass") was an obvious mid-point to connect two bridges to bring San Francisco into the modern world. But when self-styled "Norton I, Emperor of The United States," commanded his "royal subjects" to build such a bridge in 1859, his idea was but one of many that proved he was crazy. Joshua Abraham Norton (February 4, 1818-January 8, 1880) migrated to South Africa after being born in Britain to a merchant family. He later arrived in San Francisco as the 1849 Gold Rush was making headlines worldwide. During a San Francisco rice shortage in 1853, Norton moved to corner the San Francisco rice market and lost his fortune when new rice shipments suddenly arrived and rice prices crashed.

Declaring bankruptcy in 1859, he announced in the *San Francisco Bulletin* that he was the unrecognized sovereign of the United States. He had apparently lost his mind along with his riches, and the local and national news outlets played along with "Emperor Norton's" proclamations from then on. More of his "proclamations," such as dissolving the Union, ordering General Winfield Scott to march on Washington to rout legislators, and adding "Protector of Mexico" to his title, captured the attention of the national press, which encouraged him to aggrandize his celebrity. He invented an "imperial seal" to gain free meals and drink from all manner of San Francisco shops and inn keepers who welcomed his patronage. A local printing firm ran off paper currency with The Emperor's picture in uniform and royal seal displayed. Army officers at the San Francisco Presidio military base kept him well uniformed with fine trousers, a brass-buttoned jacket, a plumed hat, and a military saber.

"Norton I" became the mascot of San Francisco, followed from bar to bar by a small pack of dogs. His most famous mandate was a decree that his subjects build a bridge from San Francisco to

7. Growing Up

Oakland, which was further evidence of his lunacy but which came to pass in 1936 when the Bay Bridge was opened. Emperor Norton's title even survived into the traditional jazz age of the 1930s with a popular West Coast jazz classic called "Emperor Norton's Hunch." Mark Twain used the Emperor as a model for the King in his 1885 novel *The Adventures of Huckleberry Finn.* Norton I, Emperor of the United States and Protector of Mexico, dropped dead from a stroke in San Francisco on January 8, 1880. Ten thousand loyal San Francisco subjects paid their respects at Norton I's funeral. Local and national papers sent him off with laudatory headlines. From *The New York Times* to California's major newspapers, such comments as "No citizen of San Francisco could have been taken away who would be more generally missed" appeared.

Also within view of my bedroom window was man-made "Treasure Island," attached to the western point of Yerba Buena Island in 1936. It was completed in 1937 and intended to serve as the San Francisco airport. A change of plans led it to be the site of the Golden Gate International Exposition of 1939. I was seven years old then, living one block downhill of Coit Tower on Telegraph Hill, with my mother and father. The three of us walked for 10 minutes up the trail to the summit of Telegraph Hill to the foot of Coit Tower to view the grand opening fireworks marking the opening of the GGIE on Treasure Island. Hundreds of neighbors surrounded us, waiting for the fireworks to begin as the skies darkened.

Postcard view of the GGIE, circa 1939

This being my first view of a fireworks show, I had no idea what to expect. Treasure Island was in clear view about five miles from the viewers. My father heard some kind of a signal shot and raised me to his shoulders as the whole crowd watched the start of the amazing fireworks spectacle that seemed to last for hours. I was so excited by the fireworks that my jumping up and down so hard while sitting on dad's shoulders started to wear on him.

During the following months until September 29, 1940, my parents and I drove several times halfway across the San Francisco-Oakland Bay Bridge to visit a few of the shows and exhibitions at the GGIE until it closed 14 months before Pearl Harbor Day, December 7, 1941, which marked the start of the U.S. engagement in WWII. "Naval Station Treasure Island" became a major military base during the war by processing an average of 12,000 men per day on their way to the Pacific theater. Approximately the same number of service veterans was processed through "TI" at the war's end, returning to civilian life. Since Pearl Harbor Day fell just a few weeks before Christmas in 1941, a pall was cast over normal Christmas celebrations that holiday season.

As the pace of Naval operations in the Pacific picked up, there came a period of about three years that my view beyond my bedroom window reflected the massive investment of men, ships, equipment, and fortune that the war levied on the American economy and American families. Tens of thousands of American families' children were sent to the Pacific region to make war and defeat the enemy. On average there were two massive convoys of ships that slowly assembled in San Francisco Bay every month.

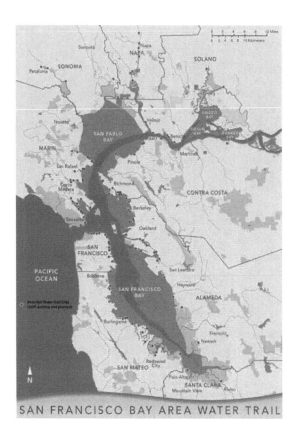

SAN FRANCISCO BAY AREA WATER TRAIL

On a Monday, I would observe a couple of destroyers and cargo ships anchored in the bay. Each following day more ships of all classes would appear moored in the bay: battle cruisers, battle ships, aircraft carriers, submarines—all being deployed to a massive flotilla; come Saturday, the convoy of ships was gone via the Golden Gate. I saw the spectacle repeated scores of times with the more somber returns of solo red-cross-emblazoned hospital ships loaded with casualties and wounded servicemen.

The first dog I ever had was named King. He was a little black and white Boston Bull Terrier that my dad brought home one day. We lived on Telegraph Hill, where a steady stream of cars loaded with tourists would drive up the hill to admire the San Francisco Bay panorama viewed from Coit Tower. Dad would entertain me by letting King grab the end of a belt in his powerful jaws while dad swung him around in a circle going faster and faster. King would never let go.

One weekend all four of us—mom, dad, myself and King—drove across town to visit my parents' good friends for an afternoon. Somehow, King made it out of their house and was nowhere to be found by the time we had to return home. It was only a 20-minute drive from one end of San Francisco to the other. But S.F. streets go up and down and around in a very complex course to get from one point to another. I cried the whole way home while my parents tried to console me. My dad would respond, "Don't worry, King will find his way home; you will see." I cried some more and prayed; I was six or seven years old. Two or three days went by and King showed up one morning, trying to wag his non-existent cropped tail. I whooped and hollered and was deliriously happy. How he navigated through the streets and hills of S.F. was a mystery to all of us.

Me with King, 1938

Months later before school started that fall, King got out of the house accidentally and went for a walk. He never ever returned. Someone in the constant streams of tourists walking around the parking lot of Coit Tower probably saw this little

7. Growing Up

"lost doggie with no ID tag on his collar" and drove home with my dog. This was conjecture, but why else would King never return home from a jaunt in his own neighborhood after demonstrating his navigational talents by returning cross town to our home?

Dad with King

The American Legacy of an Italian Motorcyclist

The tear floodgates flowed for days in spite of dad promising me that I could become a "Boy Scout" and have a lot of fun going hiking and camping, and so on...no interest. Several years passed before we got another dog, Pat, a fat black Cocker Spaniel bequeathed to us by Aunt Erma as a result of her divorce and move to Oregon. By that time, we had moved to another part of town and Pat had a dog collar with her name and address on it. Pat had a long and happy life with us.

8. Dad's Breakthrough

By 1943 my father was doing so well at his electrician's job at the shipyard that he was noticed by a civilian "naval inspector," who explained to dad what inspectors do and the pay and benefits they enjoyed. The inspector suggested that dad try out for such a position. My father followed up on the suggestion promptly and passed the interview and exam, and was hired as an Inspector of Naval Materials, a U.S. Civil Service employee.

This was a significant advancement for dad and the family, and one he took seriously and mastered, and enjoyed for many years, including several interruptions spurred by his eternal ambition, inquisitiveness, and aspiration to "make it big." My father's new eight-hour, five days-a-week job allowed more control over the family's social schedule, since mom's workdays were similarly scheduled. My elementary school years were drawing to a close and the advance to my middle school (called junior high school in California) and schedule practically coincided with the family's move to another part of town, the Portola District.

San Francisco is well known for its hilly terrain. Literally dozens of hills are scattered all over the city, no matter whether they be populated, developed, or preserved as famous landmarks that attract tourists. There are a few very flat districts of the city, such as the Sunset District in the west adjacent to the beaches, but my family always lived in the hilly areas with beautiful views and away from the normally very foggy areas adjacent to the Golden Gate and the Sunset District.

Asunta's home was on a ridge just one block above the flat valley course of a street-car route frequently smothered by dense fog day or night. When we would telephone her to chat, she could never believe our neighborhood was bright and sunny, only a 15-minute drive from hers. Many summer tourists would leave town after a short stay in some foggy area with the impression that the city was constantly shrouded in dense fog. Actually, the fog density and concentration follow a path as through a funnel whose axis travels eastward through the Golden Gate and into the bay, spilling fog up and over adjacent areas, resulting in localized chilly areas and neighborhoods. The summer fogs do not usually

8. Dad's Breakthrough

reach north of the Bay Area through Marin County or south beyond south San Francisco. Therefore, the absence of summer fogs to the north and south results in warmer climates than in the city.

In the early '50s, Nonna and Genis bought their first television set. I remember my mom making fun of their "addiction." It wasn't until much later, when I attended U.C.-Berkeley, that my parents finally broke down and got a small black and white TV of their own.

Dad's new position as an Inspector of Naval Materials meant that he would be given test samples of the variety of different metals or substances, concrete, etc., that contractors used in the finished articles. These could be components of various types of structures, armaments, ship's equipment or other supplies involved in naval operations or activities. For example, a federal contract with a manufacturer to produce an item calls for the components used in its fabrication to satisfy necessary technical specifications. Samples of the metals or materials involved in the item's fabrication must be provided to the inspector. He takes the samples to an authorized testing facility, which installs them in special machines to subject them to intense pressure, tension, or compression until they break or distort. The inspector must witness the test and report whether or not the sample passed the stress test. A failed sample test prevents the material from being used to produce the item.

My father would arrange for me to accompany him on weekends or holidays to the testing labs, foundries, and machine shops involved in the war effort's materials procurement process. Dad would proudly introduce young junior high school me to the principals involved at the firm's foundries, testing facilities, or laboratories and introduce me as "The son who is going to grow up and support me in my old age," (no pressure intended!). Dad would be given surplus or unused items, sample materials, and equipment from his friends at the inspection facilities. I would expand my "research laboratory" with the articles dad was given. My "lab" was located in the back porch of the family home. I pursued the idea of inventing "synthetic rubber," which would be a great contribution to the war effort.

The supply sources of natural rubber from the Near East were curtailed due to the war in the Pacific Ocean area. My naive dream of doing so was the result of the national news coverage of the critical role natural rubber was having upon the war effort. I thereby thought that my future education would be based upon a career involving chemistry.

Our new home near the southern perimeter of San Francisco was in a developed area adjacent to a

8. Dad's Breakthrough

very large tract of undeveloped hillsides. This was a great area for young boys to explore, construct tree-houses in the summertime, and play war games. We would build dams in uphill gullies to capture large amounts of runoff rainfall, then "bomb" the dams to unleash torrents of muddy water. This would flood the downhill streets and driveways, to the dismay of neighbors. We would have a great, non-adult-supervised time.

One of the hills in that expanse was covered in tall wild weeds that would dry out toward summer's end, providing slippery grass that my buddies and I would carefully flatten down to create a great grass-sledding run downhill for 200 yards or so; we would build the sleds with two runners covered with lengths of nailed steel strapping.

San Francisco's prominent hills almost demanded that all little boys think about building a "coaster." Kids anywhere in the hilly parts of town would build coasters out of crude lumber planks, 2x4s, ball-bearings, and a length of rope. The ends of the 2x4 front axle would be chiseled down to a cylindrical section and shaved to allow forcing a large ball-bearing onto the tip of each end of the axle to perform as a wheeled axle. The axle was then attached at its mid-point to the middle front of the plank with a bolt through its center, allowing the axle to rotate, with the steering rope attached to each end. The rear 2x4 axle, with its ball-rearing wheels at its ends, was fixed to the rear end of the uncomfortable seat plank, no brakes: voila, a coaster.

However, not at all an acceptable coaster for my father's son! Somehow, somewhere, dad found four balloon tires with ball-bearing wheels about a foot in diameter, lengths of angle-iron, a 12-inch diameter steel steering wheel with a column and rack, springs, rubber-tire inner tubes, red glass reflectors, a bit of lumber and wooden slats, nuts and bolts, and worn-out rubber sneakers. He constructed from this stuff a five-foot-long car with a cockpit, a covered "hood," a comfortably padded seat, and two plank brakes suspended by hinges forward of the steering mechanism. Rubber inner-tube loops under the seat suspended each aft-end of the long brake-pedal planks, whose bottoms had a tennis-shoe each nailed to the rear bottom ends of each long "brake pedal": the braking powered by the driver stomping down upon the suspended ends of the pedals forward of the driver's seat. Several pairs of old tennis-shoe brakes were worn out after the few years of coaster season.

This vehicle made me "king of the hill": downhill-powered by gravity, and uphill-powered by a pal or pals with me still steering and riding, being pushed back up to the top of the hill: the pushers would then be allowed to take a solo drive back downhill. There were plenty of pushers to choose from, so I was a very popular kid.

8. Dad's Breakthrough

The only thing that kept me or any of my pals from being killed at the intersections was that in between each steep block of a hill would be a relatively flat block of homes, so that with enough momentum my coaster would have enough speed left over to carry me to the top of the next downhill block. The whole range of city blocks in the neighborhood comprised three to four downhill blocks of homes with intervening blocks of relatively flat grades.

None of my pals' ball-bearing plank scooters could build up enough speed to carry them beyond a few homes on the flat stretches. Also, in those WWII years, rare was the home that had two automobiles. Many had none and auto traffic was light and fairly restricted to going to and from work. Nonetheless, the kids were not completely crazy. I would station my ball-bearing equipped coaster cohorts along the route; everyone who wanted a turn at the wheel of my balloon-tired "racing roadster" would post himself at every intersection to warn me, or the driver of an infrequent automobile, of a possible problem.

Warning of an oncoming vehicle would require plenty of downhill braking. We never mentioned to our parents exactly what we were doing, but excellent public transportation, light traffic, and luck helped us avoid injuries and survive the thrills of down-hill coasting in the "hilly city by the bay." Reflecting upon my childhood now it is quite clear to me that I had been, inevitably and unconsciously, inheriting my father's traits: curiosity, risk-taking, adventure, luck, and trusting my friends.

In spite of occasional high-pitched arguments, particularly when my dad embarked on his occasional attempts to start some new venture, my parents were in love forever. Dad was adventurous until his later years but was always proud of mom and respected her. They enjoyed cuddling on the living room couch together as we listened to all the comical radio programs before the advent of WWII and television; the voices of Red Skelton, Fibber McGee and Molly, Abbott and Costello, Fred Allen, Amos 'n' Andy, and the Edgar Bergen-Charlie McCarthy show often filled our house. I remember playing the popular kids' games of the time, including dominoes, Chinese checkers, Monopoly, Casino, and solitaire.

9. Cleopatra's Victory Garden

Nationwide rationing for gasoline and food went into effect in 1942 soon after Pearl Harbor Day of December 7, 1941. Any individual and family who had their own yard or garden soon found it desirable to learn the basics of planting and cultivating some kinds of vegetables. Or better yet, if your community or neighborhood permitted raising chickens or rabbits, and if you had a child who would enthusiastically learn and help, it would be easier.

The family "Victory Garden" that practically every San Francisco citizen created in his or her back yard during World War II pretty soon alleviated rationing anxieties, improved morale, strengthened feelings of patriotism, and made the citizenry feel that we were "supporting the troops."

The home that we moved to in early 1942 in the southeast sector of San Francisco was so blessed. Soon after moving in, my parents appreciated the possibilities of our own back yard to do all of the above. For some reason dad decided a high priority was to acquire a goat, and I was excited about the prospect. So, dad designed a very nice goat shed about four feet wide by six feet long and five feet high with a tarpaper-protected planked roof and a hinged door and planked floor.

In June 1942 we completed the goat shed. The backyards of all the homes in our neighborhood were 30 feet wide and 60 feet deep. We located the shed within 20 feet of the rear fence of our home's property, which would soon adjoin the backyard of a new home behind and uphill from ours. The shed's location allowed for six vegetable plots between the rear of our home and the completely fenced-in yard.

With the goat shed completed, my father and I spent a weekend driving around the countryside south of San Francisco searching for a goat. Dad's research and our car travel up and down the peninsula yielded no goat. Several weeks later that summer a large two-story home appeared, being towed up the steep hill in its entirety through the intersection at the foot of our street; then, continuing up the hill it was hauled and turned left at the next street above our home. It was finally deposited on the lot directly behind our home and the common fence.

9. Cleopatra's Victory Garden

Dad of course welcomed the new neighbors soon after they occupied their "new" home with a bottle of wine. He returned and announced that they would be bringing their large collection of rabbits to their new Victory Garden and had asked my father if he would like one of their rabbits. The goat shed issue was resolved. During the following week we converted it to a large complex of eight smaller rabbit apartments with a common wire mesh to let their droppings fall to the floor beneath, which I had the pleasure of shoveling regularly to fertilize our farm.

Nobody ever asked my father why in the world he aspired to own a goat as part of our WWII Victory Garden efforts. I just took it for granted that it would be fun, with no concern about what we would "do" with it. Dad was always coming up with curious interests and projects. Mom never questioned his intentions or plans about the goat. We already had another dog, so one more pet was no big deal. Once the alternative appeared—to convert the goat shed to rabbit hutches—he just seized upon the remodeling effort as another fun task.

A rabbit's hutch-warming was conducted on the arrival of "Cleopatra," a very large and fat (we thought) gray and white female, who we discovered to be pregnant a few weeks later. She became a fecund momma over the years, with the help from time to time of our neighbor's "Mister" Cleopatra.

Over the years, we built a rabbit hutch complex that housed up to 30 bunnies, which, upon being ready for the table, provided more than enough protein for several growing kids in the neighborhood beyond the meager amount allowed by the ration books.

We were very patriotic. In spite of the space required by the rabbit hutches and vegetable plots at the end of the garden, there was still ample room for a sizable chicken coop for over a dozen Rhode Island Reds and White Leghorns and a stone barbecue pit with an adjustable grill, picnic table, and benches, all of which dad designed and built with my help.

Me and Aunt Olga with the grill

9. Cleopatra's Victory Garden

Maintenance and feeding the menagerie eventually grew to a burden for me but it was a war effort and who else was available to do it since mom and dad were working full time? But one task I was spared from or even witnessing was the killing of my pets! Dad always gave me some distracting chore to do, or I knew what was going on and made myself scarce when it was time to kill and butcher a rabbit or chicken. We never made a big deal about it. He never invited me to learn how to do it and I avoided the opportunity. I could see where he set up to do it, out of sight of the rabbit hutches and chicken coops; and I pretended not to know or care what he was doing.

The Victory Garden and Farm grew to be the finest and most well-appointed outdoor picnic party spot in the neighborhood. My parents worked hard during the week at their regular jobs, but there was plenty of work to tend to it all, and I was expected to toe the line and not stint on all the attendant home and garden chores year-round.

There nonetheless was time, particularly during the summers and after school hours, for me to goof off, including coaxing my buddies to "help" in the Victory Garden. I particularly enjoyed teaching my pals when collecting the daily egg production from the hens how to eat a warm, freshly laid raw egg. Dad taught me how to do it. Once mastered, it was a great way for me to gross out my pals. It went like this: you select a nice warm large egg from the nest, rinse it off quickly under a water tap, punch a small hole in each end of the eggshell, and suck out the raw egg—wonderful! If my buddies thought it gross, I could label them cowards or worse. All it took was one of the kids to accept the challenge and they would all be compelled to do it or else! I now wonder if they ever told their parents how brave they were. This was an early lesson in peer pressure.

Being an only child, I was, on occasion during my youth, chided as being spoiled or particularly privileged by my parents. I actually never thought I was receiving any special treatment. I was given household, yard, and garden maintenance chores and was expected to fulfill my duties. I never thought of complaining about scrubbing bathroom floors on all fours, keeping my room tidy, and helping out with special tasks. On the few occasions when I overlooked a regular chore, or did it late, dad would not fail to punish me, using "the rod"—with traditional Italian temper and fashion.

The WWII years were notable for children, not only because of food rationing and constant reminders of combat fatalities marked by window stickers on families' homes but by a pandemic. It was called polio, and particularly targeted children. Photographs of children in an "iron lung" were commonly published in the newspapers, and children were warned to avoid public swimming pools. In large cities such as San Francisco, such facilities were the only way for a child to be exposed to swimming or learn about the sport during the summer. No responsible parents would allow their child to frequent such public facilities. An occasional opportunity for me to learn to swim during my middle- and high-school years was on the Russian River where Genis Mayolas, my mothero's stepfather, had built a summer cottage.

Mom's younger sister Olga and her husband, Johnny, were proficient swimmers who made swimming in the Russian River look so easy that I would just walk into the river on a few occasions and practically drown before reaching the float about 25 feet away off the river bank. I naturally grew to have a fear of the water until becoming a freshman at the University of California, Berkeley. All freshmen were encouraged by the welcoming faculty to take any kind of non-credit sport for the sake of "good health." I dutifully spent two semesters of my freshman year taking swimming lessons at 8 o'clock in the morning three times weekly, which meant I commuted from San Francisco at 6 a.m. The swimming instructors taught their students every stroke of the sport, including diving, lifesaving, and water polo. I managed to change my fear of the water to a healthy respect for it and would always be a "sinker" and not a natural "floater," possibly due to sharing a very lean physiognomy with dad.

I was the ring bearer at Aunt Olga and Johnny Risso's wedding in 1939 in San Francisco. Johnny and Olga had been childhood sweethearts at Balboa High School and spent scant time as newlyweds before Pearl Harbor and the U.S. entry to WWII.

Aunt Olga and Uncle Johnny's wedding portrait

Johnny served in the Army Air Forces long before it became a separate branch of the U.S. Armed

Forces. He became an Army Air Forces Glider Crew Chief, eventually stationed in Britain, and was involved in the invasion of the French coast after D-Day. I was a proud 10- to 12-year-old at the time and corresponded with Johnny regularly, exchanging letters in the officially allowed "V-Mail" flimsy stationery. The letters were subject to inspection and censorship to ensure that no sensitive information would be disclosed in correspondence between servicemen or -women and the public. Uncle John and Aunt Olga had two children—Elaine and Nancy—while Johnny was in the service, my two American cousins.

Me as ring-bearer

The American Legacy of an Italian Motorcyclist

When Uncle Johnny returned from WWII, he and Aunt Olga, mom's youngest sister, established their permanent residency in the large home that Nonna Asunta had acquired after her divorce from Primo several years earlier. Uncle Johnny's hobby was photography, and, helped by Asunta's second husband, Genis, Johnny converted a corner space in the basement into a well-equipped darkroom with the proper lighting and running water. Johnny filled the room with all the necessary developing, enlarging, printing, and drying paraphernalia. He eventually taught me how to develop, enlarge, and print photos taken with my dad's bellows-type of early Kodak camera. I never became committed to the hobby, but it was a lot of fun to get one of my girlfriends at the time to help me out when the lights had to be dimmed to allow things to be developed. And Nonna was always occupied upstairs in her kitchen when we would be invited up for lunch or a snack.

10. Italian Army POWs

During WWII my father worried about his family in Italy, caught up in the midst of a war that had little comparison with the world war dad had managed to survive. My father was particularly concerned about his brother Maso, having been notified in pre-war letters from his parents that Maso had graduated and become a physician. After several years of practicing medicine, he had been inducted to the Italian Army and dispatched to North Africa as a member of the Italian Army, whose mission was to establish an Italian colony in Ethiopia. This was a pipe dream of Mussolini's that was quite unpopular with most Italians.

The American press followed the campaign of the Italian Army and thoroughly reported its defeat by the Ethiopian Army and allied British Army in early 1940. The majority of the Italian Army was captured and imprisoned by the British Army, but no specific details regarding Italian Army casualties were available. Dad assumed the worst and hoped for the best regarding Maso's fate, let alone the fate of the rest of his Italian family. By 1941 a very large Italian prisoner of war (POW) camp was established in Oakland, right across the bay, easily accessible by driving across the San Francisco-Oakland Bay Bridge. Dad discovered that any American citizen in good standing might apply to the POW camp administration, in person, for permission to not only visit the POWs but invite them for daylong visits with the citizen's family. By then it was quite clear to the American populace and the POW community that Mussolini's regime was living on borrowed time, particularly considering that Italy was on its way to becoming an ally of the U.S. after the invasion of Sicily and the Italian peninsula itself.

My father took me with him on numerous visits to the Oakland POW camp for the primary purpose of finding out if Maso was there or if any prisoner there had ever heard of him or anything about him. The procedure was to register at the camp's entrance and request to visit specific barracks of prisoners from certain Italian provinces who spoke the same dialect. The entire Italian Army was geographically organized to ensure that the chain of verbal communication and command could be accurately understood, from the upper echelons to the lowest in the chain. Italy had existed as a coherent nation for far less than a century, formed by the unification of over a dozen principalities, all speaking different languages. For example, my father and his family could understand very little of a Sicilian citizen's speech. The further away principalities were located from one another, the more pronounced were their different dialects and written communication.

We would then be escorted to the appropriate barrack, where we would be left to introduce ourselves to the unit commander. After lengthy conversations with each barrack commander, dad would reach the same conclusion: no one had ever known or heard anything about Dottore Maso Paredi. We always returned home, however, with at least one prisoner/guest for a welcome exchange and the fine Italian meal that my parents had prepared, and the POWs were always returned to their barracks on time.

These POW visits were also providing me with the opportunity, unappreciated until later in life, to "learn Italian"! Dad and other Italian hosts of these POW interactions suspected that the government's purpose in establishing the liberal policy with the POWs was to keep their morale up and expose them to the American way of life. We even learned from a few of the POWs that some Italian-American families with daughters of marriageable age gained Italian POW sons-in-law after their daughters developed romantic relations with a few very lucky guests after several dinner engagements.

The American Legacy of an Italian Motorcyclist

11. Heroic Survivors

My father lost track of his family in Italy as soon as WWII drew the U.S. into active engagement with its European allies. From 1939 until the fall of Nazi Germany in 1944 there was no regular international mail service between the U.S. and any European countries. Dad had no idea how, or if, his parents or any of his siblings had survived the calamity. He only began to get letters from his family in 1944. His parents had survived but not without extremely traumatic interludes. As American troops advanced up the Italian peninsula with its Italian Army allies, the Italian public had to be extremely careful. The very extensive and active Italian guerrilla organization made it its business to harass the retreating German forces. German forces were targeted by the well-armed Italian "partisans," young and old, who had no sympathy for the German troops retreating in disarray. The partisans would kill German soldiers at every opportunity. In the latter stages of the German retreat, their forces grew weak and disorganized, making themselves extremely vulnerable to the emboldened guerrilla fighters.

The German army retreat finally reached the area of dad's parents' town, Boves, Piedmonte. Four German soldiers seeking food had been captured by a partisan group. The partisans took food and the four German captives to the nearby mountains. The German commander gave the Italian civilians a two-hour deadline to go to the mountains and return with the four German captives. In the meantime, the German commander had his troops round up as many Boves citizens as possible and assemble them in a location to observe the execution of a dozen elder male Boves citizens if the two-hour deadline were to expire. The group to be executed included my grandfather: my father's father, Ercole. Someone in the crowd of observers shouted out in Italian, "You can't shoot Ercole Paredi; he is the Mayor of Boves!"

The German firing-squad commander unceremoniously released Ercole from the lineup and substituted the complaining hero, who was executed in Ercole's place when the two-hour deadline expired. The town was then destroyed by the German army's flame-throwing operation and photos of the destruction were carried by news outlets worldwide.

11. Heroic Survivors

Report Nazis Wipe Out Italian Village

NEW YORK, Oct. 26 (AP).—A dispatch to the Columbia Broadcasting System today from the European continent, quoting diplomatic informants, said that enraged German troops wiped out an entire Italian village of 2,000 "in the same manner that they destroyed Lidice," in Czechoslovakia.

NEAR FRENCH BORDER

The account said the Italian Alpine village of Boves, near the French border, was leveled by flame throwers. It continued:

Italian Alpine guerrilla fighters—warring on the German occupation forces—visited Boves in quest of food. The patriots easily overwhelmed the few German troops in the villages and carried four of the Germans away to the mountains as hostages.

Within a few hours a German motorized detachment arrived in Boves from Turin. The German commander called in the local priest and told him he would give the populace two hours to go into the mountains and bring back the four German soldiers.

TIME TOO SHORT

The people of Boves tried to make contact with the guerrillas, but the time was too short. The deadline expired and the German commander ordered a flame-throwing detachment into action. Every house in the village was set afire, and two hours later Boves was a smoldering ruin.

Yanks Hit Burma, Indo-China Japs

CHUNGKING, Oct. 26 (AP).— American bombers based in China have struck heavy blows at the Japanese in Burma and Indo-China to support Chinese ground troops, a communique from Lieutenant General Joseph W. Stilwell's headquarters announced today.

121

The American Legacy of an Italian Motorcyclist

Lucia and Ercole Paredi

122

11. Heroic Survivors

The fates of the four German army prisoners who were abducted from Boves by Italian partisans leading to the destruction of the town are unknown. Considering that their abductors were probably aware of what happened in Boves and other factors, they were more than likely killed. Their fates were never reported by the press.

My father heard about the incident and other similar ones on his first trip to Italy after the war to find out what had happened to his family. To facilitate several trips to Italy, he joined the Zappettini Travel Agency in North Beach, well-known by the local Italian community. He resigned his Civil Service job to do so and my mother, understandably, resigned herself to his decision, which was primarily motivated to support his Italian family.

Dad found that his two sisters had also survived. The eldest, Maria, had never married but had had an illegitimate child, Sandro, presumably by a German soldier, and eventually continued her professorship in French language and history at the University of Torino. Dad's sister Franca married an Italian insurance executive, continued in her job teaching higher mathematics at the University in Milan, and had a daughter, Silvia.

My father's younger brother, Maso, on the other hand, survived his Italian army sojourn by undergoing a most extraordinary odyssey. Maso had indeed been drafted to serve with the Italian Army in Ethiopia as a medical officer. He was eventually captured with the rest of the army in the area surrounding Addis Ababa by the British forces in eastern North Africa in 1940. And then he escaped, solo.

The only facts about Maso's escape were known because of my father's meeting with Maso in the course of the first trip dad made to Italy after the war. Maso told my father that he escaped the British POW camp by himself and proceeded on foot with few resources, traversing Eastern Europe on an extended northward journey until he reached his parents' home in Boves in the dark of night.

Ercole and Lucia were astonished to see their long-lost son alive after years of assuming the worst. Maso's unexpected arrival was undoubtedly a massive shock, surprise, and relief; and his welcome home meal in the middle of the night was hurried. They immediately realized the sensitivity of their new situation: it must be kept perfectly secret, not to be revealed to anyone, not the neighbors, not the joy of his return, but also presented a serious problem. After the quick meal and a family discussion, the three of them determined to take every measure to conceal Maso's arrival and presence until the war was over. His parents undertook the clandestine project of

11. Heroic Survivors

feeding, clothing, and sheltering Maso for the indefinite conclusion of the war.

The facts were that Maso still was an Italian army officer and might be considered a deserter. As a physician he would have been an important asset to the resistance fighters. He had no desire to be an intelligence asset to the Allies. There was no better place to hide than to stay in place. Ercole and Maso grabbed shovels and quietly dug a hole in the garden behind the home, scattered the earth, and found a section of corrugated sheet metal roofing to cover the hole of Maso's temporary shelter for daylight hours of sleep, recovery, and rest. Until the guerrillas shot, killed, and hanged Mussolini and his mistress, Clara Petachi, not far away near Milan and the German soldiers were long gone were the Paredis' complete family and neighbors to realize that Maso had survived and returned.

After WWII ended, my parents took me at the age of 16 to Italy. Among many family visits, one day they introduced me to my Uncle Maso, in a gathering of only five others of my father's family. We knew that Maso had been captured by the British Army in 1940 and shortly thereafter escaped imprisonment in Ethiopia, eventually appearing at his parents' home in Boves in 1944. One can therefore conclude that Maso's odyssey lasted as long as four years, between his escape from Ethiopia to his escape from the hole in his

125

parents' garden. So, when I met my Uncle Maso in the presence of both his parents and mine, I observed a well-dressed, slight, quiet-spoken, introverted chain-smoker; a man of few words with a rueful smile and a fidgety demeanor.

How was I, a callow 16 year old, to open up a conversation with this mythic man after seeing the hole in the ground he essentially lived in until the war was over. How could I say anything but "Molto piacere, Zio Maso" ("Much pleasure, Uncle Maso")? The medical terms of Maso's possible condition evolved over the many wars between my father's and my lifetime from "shell-shock" to "battle fatigue" to "post-traumatic shock syndrome" (PTSD). In retrospect, I now assume that Maso suffered from any or all of them. Dad probably never asked his brother, Maso, for any details of his odyssey. Maso probably never volunteered the details of his trek from Ethiopia to Boves with anyone.

Had Maso ever divulged the details of his solo escape to my father, he would have shared at least a summary of it with me; he never did. I had no doubt that Maso never shared a word of his ordeal, particularly with his wife or daughter. The latter, one of my two Italian female cousins, Louisanna, with my other female Italian cousin, Silvia, attended my wedding in England several years later. Uncle Maso died in his late 50s. It would appear that my father and his family collectively suffered, one way or another, due to the wars, each time believing at the time that this had been "the war to end all wars": dad, from four years of luckily navigating no-man's lands on a motorcycle; his father, Ercole, from escaping a firing squad death, thanks to another hero taking his place; dad's sister, Maria, bearing an illegitimate son; and dad's brother, Maso, escaping capture in Ethiopia by virtue of a solo years-long mysterious trek, on foot, to his parents' home in northwestern Italy—heroes, all of them, by one definition or another.

Maso Paredi, circa 1970

The American Legacy of an Italian Motorcyclist

12. The Trumpeter

The fall of 1943 began my first year at San Francisco's Portola Junior High School. The school's principal welcomed all the boys and girls on our first day there and went on to explain we would be able to enroll in one of two electives. Asking us to raise our hands as he announced the two choices, the first mentioned was typing and every one of the girls' hands went up. Upon his announcement of the second elective, band, all the boys' hands were raised.

The first day in the band room, Mr. Leek, the band teacher, asked which of the boys wanted to be in each of the several instrument sections of the band. For some reason I chose the trumpet section and all the other sections, from clarinets all the way to the percussion section, were filled. I took to the trumpet like a duck to water.

The dynamics of trumpet playing and piano playing made a big difference to me, given that I

129

did not have a little finger on my left hand. The non-dominant hand of a trumpeter only supports the horn and pulls the horn back onto the lips of the musician with varying pressure: the higher the note, the more pressure, the lower the note, the less pressure. The non-dominant hand must have a thumb and at least two or three fingers to securely support the horn and constantly vary the pressure of the horn's mouthpiece upon the lips. The three middle fingers of the dominant hand rest upon the tops of each valve and push down in different combinations to produce different notes of the musical scale. Attached to the side of each valve's cylinder is an extra length of tubing which forces the trumpeter's breath to follow a longer path through the "main length" of the trumpet: the longer the path, the lower pitch of the note. The development of the trumpet followed that of the steam engine, when tiny valves patterned after the steam engine were added to the bugle. The different notes that a bugler makes are restricted to one key (Concert Bb or C) and each note is produced by a different pressure applied by the bugler between his lips and the instrument's mouthpiece. A bugler need only have one arm with a hand capable of holding the instrument and pulling it against his lips to produce bugle calls.

By the end of the first semester I was qualified to take private trumpet lessons from Mr. Leek weekly, downtown in the basement of the Golden Gate

12. The Trumpeter

Music Store. My parents, particularly my mother, were quite pleased to see my enthusiasm for any kind of music since I had lost interest in the piano.

My first public performance, Portola Junior High, 1944

Not too long after my enthusiastic embrace of the trumpet, mom and I were playing duets of popular and classical compositions. My parents were both thrilled with my interest and ability with the horn. Mom never gave up the piano and practiced faithfully and performed regularly for church and ladies clubs into her 80s.

The American Legacy of an Italian Motorcyclist

Six months of private lessons from Mr. Leek showed the junior high school music teacher that I should advance my mastery of the trumpet by taking private lessons from a professional musician, Mr. Orlando Giosi, trombonist for the San Francisco Symphony, who accepted me as a private student. For several years every Saturday I would take public transportation from home to Mr. Giosi's residence. The trip was about an hour each way by three buses and a streetcar. Through the remaining two years of junior high school and five years of high school I spent every possible Saturday going back and forth to Mr. Giosi's home for private trumpet lessons. I was the only kid on block to practice the trumpet. But other kids were practicing the trombone, drums, etc. I never knew our neighbors to complain. I suppose they were at work while we were practicing.

I joined the nearby Daly City Concert Band's trumpet section and a teenage swing band composed of high school students from a public high school. On completing junior high school, I entered a private vocational and college preparatory high school with no music department called Lick-Wilmerding High School (LWHS). That private high school would today be classified as a scientific, technical, engineering, and mathematics (STEM) school. It has grown over the years and evolved into the finest coeducational high school in the Bay Area. One of my most memorable accomplishments at LWHS was reading—and thoroughly enjoying—Tolstoy's *War and Peace,* to the wonder of my English and French teacher, Miss French.

I had two teachers at LWHS who were especially influential. Miss French, my very pretty blond professor of French Language and English, was one. Her students were all in the college preparatory curriculum at LWHS (versus the vocational prep students). Miss French's primary goal as an English teacher was to have every one of her college prep students pass the English language entrance exams at U.C.-Berkeley and Stanford. Every entering freshman at U.C.-Berkeley was required to take the English Entry Exam and pass it. Failure to do so would require the student to retake the two-unit course repeatedly, non-credit, every semester, until the student was able to retake the test and pass it, no credit given any semester for the course. Failure to pass the test would prevent the student from receiving a diploma and graduating from U.C.-Berkeley. One of my frat brothers retook the course every semester, eight times, and never passed it. He never received a diploma. He was a great pianist, however, and the pianist in my trio in the fraternity. Go figure!

The other teacher who I remember vividly was Mr. Tibbets, who taught Chemistry and Earth Sciences. Mr. Tibbets was a real character, quite elderly in the eyes of his students, a big man somewhat sloppily dressed, never close shaven, full head of disheveled hair, a gruff and intimidating voice and almost menacing presence. He really knew his stuff and helped me a lot when I had to remain an extra year at LWHS just to take the two-unit course in Civics in the next year's spring semester. The earth sciences he taught me in all that extra time heavily influenced me to change my major from chemistry to petroleum engineering at U.C.-Berkeley.

San Francisco has a very large Irish community, so St. Patrick's Day was a major event, with a huge hours-long parade of bands, community organizations, female baton twirlers, and horse troops and horse clubs from all over the state. In my junior and high school years I became the strongest first-position trumpet member of the Daly City Municipal Band, which was composed of about 40 members, consisting of a few adults but mostly students of high schools and local universities. The parade started from the San Francisco Ferry Building, a historic structure at the beginning of Market Street, which long before then was the major terminal of the large ferry fleet connecting San Francisco to the East Bay. With the advent of the two major bridges and then airports, the ferry boats were scuttled. The Ferry Building today is essentially a museum, but marks the most commercially important site of early San

12. The Trumpeter

Francisco history and is a very prominent edifice, with its huge clock at the foot of Market Street and its back to the bay.

The St. Patrick's Day Parade was one of three major annual events that the DCMB performed. The parade was unique because all the bands that contributed to the spectacle were probably outnumbered by the vast number of beautiful horses with their extravagantly costumed riders. They would always steal the show but leave behind voluminous evidence of their proud prancing. Marching bands practice as much precision marching as they do practicing their charts of music for the occasion. The discipline of straight ranks and lines of musicians with their eyes only partly on their charts and otherwise focused on the array of "horse apples" on the roads provided as much entertainment to spectators as the music.

The DCMB was also the official band of the Napa Valley State Fair, held every summer at the Napa Fairgrounds, which thankfully required no marching but instead involved seated performances twice daily for three or four days. Another yearly event was held at San Francisco's Kezar Football Stadium for the popular "East-West Professional Football Championship" game. The DCMB was seated in the end zone and played during the arrival of spectators coming to observe the annual contest between the two football teams: one representing the East and the other representing the West; both teams were composed of all-star professional football players from various teams from each American zone. In September 1946, the stadium was reopened as the home of the San Francisco 49ers professional football team.

My commitment to music and the trumpet never flagged. Mr. Giosi, during my high school years, seconded me to the San Francisco Junior Symphony. I was also a member of a German Brass Concert Band. Practically all of the young musicians who I performed with in a variety of bands were older than I was. A few of them became old enough to apply to join the U.S. Marine Corps Reserves on Treasure Island, which had a terrific band. The prospects of joining the corps and qualifying to join the band were very tempting to me at a time when the Korean War had not yet involved the United States. Three or four of the older boys yielded to the idea of being able to qualify and be accepted to the band, and talked their parents into allowing them to join the Marine Corps Reserves with the objective to qualify for entry to the U.S. Marine Corps Reserves Band. Their parents supported their ambitions, and the young men joined the USMC Reserves.

I was impressed by their ambition and success in following their dream. However, my father could smell a war developing from a great distance. When I mentioned the "success" of my musician pals to dad and shared with him my own thoughts of following suit in the next year or two, dad poured very cold water over that idea and explained his reasoning. The Korean War involving the U.S. and every branch of its military officially was launched in 1950. My pals ended up with the U.S. Marine Corps soon thereafter, carrying Browning Automatic Rifles (BARs) instead of saxophones or trombones. One of those young Marines never returned.

During those early years, as I studied music and joined several different types of bands, my father tired of driving me and my buddy musicians to and from rehearsals or gigs. Dad therefore decided it was time for him to teach me to drive the family's four-door Hudson sedan. It, as mostly all automobiles then, had no automatic transmission, no power steering or power brakes, etc.

Often after my private music lessons at Mr. Giosi's residence, dad would meet me and we'd drive to Lake Merced Park near the San Francisco oceanfront. Traffic there was minimal on Saturday afternoons, a perfect place for dad to teach me how to drive. It was fun but nerve-wracking for both of us. While the Lake Merced roads and area were very flat, once out in the hilly part of the city the coordination of hands and feet to hold the car at rest on a steep hill while waiting for a traffic light to change was a real challenge. My father was a driving-safety fanatic and the first time at Lake

Merced Park that he shouted out "STOP!" I leisurely came to a stop and was severely rebuked by dad screaming, "Is that how you would stop if a kid ran out of that driveway chasing a ball?" Nonetheless, he trusted me eventually and implicitly after I got my first driver's license at 17 to take the family car, the only car, to anyplace, anytime. That marked my liberation from childhood and introduction to young adulthood.

Me and my parents

13. A Golden Opportunity

Dad's frequent travel agent-facilitated trips to Italy in the post-war years afforded him not only valued time with his Italian family but an awareness of the moribund state of Italian industry and economy. Remembering his post-WWI experiences, the state of the shipping industry particularly came to mind. He started to make Italian contacts in that sector and was quick to discover that the Italian merchant fleet had been devastated. It needed ships of every description.

My father's experience working with and for the U.S. Navy prior to and during WWII reminded him that scores of war-related naval equipment, from warships to anything else that floated, were to become available and sold off in the U.S. civilian marketplace. He met with several principals in Italy in the maritime trade to understand what they would find of most interest to obtain from the U.S. surplus war-matériel market. The results of

139

those discussions led dad to approach several of his San Francisco acquaintances to propose possible investment opportunities. My father's idea was to purchase a surplus military ship to resell to Italian investors.

Bingo: Dad immediately visualized his position in such a group of investors in the San Francisco Bay area, and he had already established a group of prospective Italian maritime community developers. One of the first steps was to sell the idea to prospective investors, and dad had no trouble in identifying prospects and promoting the idea. He was in a great position to put the whole thing together, connecting the supply to the demand. My father had no intention or ability to fund any part of such a venture. But he would have the time, energy, and knowledge that the American investment prospects would need. All they had to do was provide funds to support such a project, with dad working for nothing but managing both ends of the activity and sharing in the Italian sale proceeds if the numbers worked.

My mother was skeptical and thought the idea crazy, but dad convinced her that it was a cinch and the prospective profits to the investors and his share of a sale in Italy presented few risks but great rewards to themselves. Mom argued that he should return to working for the U.S. Navy as part of the Civil Service and reminded dad that one of the prospective partners had a bad reputation in

13. A Golden Opportunity

San Francisco. At 15, I had nothing to offer at that stage and was heavily involved in high school academics and musical activities.

The time arrived to survey the surplus ships, moored gunnel-to-gunnel in a huge surplus ship anchorage far up the San Francisco Bay called Bodega Bay. Dad got the approval from the newly established investment partnership to undertake such a survey and report back to its members with his recommendations. Dad made the appointment to visit the large fleet of all kinds of former U.S. Navy vessels, already declared surplus and available for sale to the highest bidders.

One Saturday dad took me with him to spend the day hopping from one ship's gunnel to another to gain an idea of what was available within the kind of budget delineated by the partnership. The final selection of a ship was left up to my father. He selected a brand-new "anti-submarine net-tender" that had only recently undertaken its maiden voyage to Hawaii and back to prove itself seaworthy, navigable, and ready for war deployment. A net-tender is a ship 240 feet in length, 40 feet in beam, double-oak hull, propelled by a single propeller, with an engine room of two gigantic "BUDA" diesel engines that drive electrical generators to power electrical motors that drive the propeller. The ship would normally have a crew of six officers and 30 crewmen to carry out its military mission. Its vast holds stored huge

141

quantities of rope nets, cables, and deployment tackle to set the nets underwater to prevent enemy subs from entering harbors of U.S. Navy warships. It was fully equipped to accomplish its mission and had scores of steel chests containing two carefully wrapped spare parts for every rotating piece of equipment onboard, radar and advanced communication gear. It cost the U.S. $1,300,000 to build.

The partnership dad marshaled placed a bid of $30,000 for the ship and was awarded its title. The partnership took ownership of the vessel and it was sailed to the San Francisco Hunters Point Naval Shipyard in the spring of 1948 to be prepared for its departure to Genoa the coming fall. Minor modifications to the ship were made to remove two large bow-mounted projecting towers to manage net deployment, and the holds were emptied of all the spare equipment and sold.

My father managed all the activities at the shipyard and I assisted him that summer to empty all the crew quarters of lockers for the 30-man crew and officers' quarters. Many square yards of heavy canvas were purchased and deployed in all the vacated holds up to the gunnels, where continuous space between the two hulls of the ship was designed to allow sea water washing over the deck in heavy seas to flow down between the two hulls, reaching the bilge and from there pumped by the bilge pumps back to the sea. The sea water was presumed to be free of any large quantities of matter that might foul the bilge pumps, which would render them useless. The purpose of installing the canvas was to prevent the chosen one-way cargo of coke, necessary to serve as ballast, to accidentally shift during any extremely rough seas and foul the bilge pumps. The choice of coke to serve as ballast on the one-way trip to Genoa was a reasonable idea because it was a vital ingredient in the production of steel; Italian steel mills would purchase it and the proceeds would be applied to pay expenses of the ship's transport.

While the ship was being stripped of its war-related gear and equipment at Hunters Point Naval Shipyard, the news reached the local Italian community that its ultimate destination was Genoa, Italy. The project manager's name, Giovanni "Nino" Paredi, also quickly became known to numerous Italian immigrants in San Francisco as the man to approach to consider including in the ship's cargo clothing and other items destined for their surviving families all over Italy.

Phone calls started to pour in and dad could not say no. He agreed to accept such items, and cash, to distribute to the callers' families. He agreed to pack and see to the delivery of all items to scores of family members of those who had immigrated to San Francisco whose families had remained in Italy, had survived the war, but needed help.

During that summer of 1948 dad arranged to use space in the local church hall to receive voluminous quantities of all donations, including $30,000 in cash, to be disbursed to the many addressees. My parents and I spent weeks receiving, inventorying, and labeling hundreds of items, packing them in special wooden boxes, called tea-boxes. These boxes would have been discarded by the tea importing companies that regularly received large volumes of unprocessed tea leaves, whose raw products from foreign locations would arrive at San Francisco bay dockage facilities. The boxes of donations were carefully stenciled with the names and addresses of every recipient.

My father kept the ledger listing how much cash would be delivered to each recipient of the goods. One of the investment group partners, "Captain Terry," volunteered to upgrade his First-Mate Certificate to a Captain's Certificate to command the ship on its one-way voyage to Genoa. Dad and Captain Terry interviewed and hired six crewmen to help the Captain operate and navigate the *Santa Lucia* (rechristened after my grandmother's name, Lucia) from San Francisco through the Panama Canal, the Gulf of Mexico, and on across the Atlantic, through the Mediterranean Sea, to the port of Genoa.

13. A Golden Opportunity

Renzo Turco, Captain Terry, and Dad on the *Santa Lucia*

I dearly wished to be included in the crew, but dad refused to consider my offer in no uncertain terms. The departure of the *Santa Lucia* was arranged to allow for its arrival in Genoa early in 1949. Dad accompanied me to a meeting with my high school principal to request a short leave-of-absence for me to extend the school's 1948 Christmas holiday, permitting me to accompany my parents' trip to Genoa and get back to school for the opening of the spring semester. I was given the extra time, providing I took all my books with me and passed all the tests I would be unable to take due to my absence.

145

The American Legacy of an Italian Motorcyclist

Me on the *Santa Lucia*, 1948

I was the top student in my class, the student body president, and was permitted the extra time. It was to be my first time out of California, allowing me to be introduced to all of my Italian family. When the time came in mid-December, my parents and I boarded the "City of San Francisco" train in Oakland. It took three days to arrive in New York City and board the steamship for Genoa. Dad was to remain in Italy to conclude the sale of the *Santa Lucia*. My mother and I would return to San Francisco in time for me to finish my senior year at

13. A Golden Opportunity

Lick-Wilmerding High School, graduate in June 1949, and enter the University of California, Berkeley, that fall.

The *Santa Lucia* steaming out of San Francisco Harbor

The American Legacy of an Italian Motorcyclist

14. All Aboard!

After many months of planning and preparation, my parents and I took the train, the "City of San Francisco," from Oakland to New York City for three nights and days, stopping only for fuel.

The "City of San Francisco"

During every daylight hour I had my eyes glued to the windows of our cabin. To this day visions come to my mind of the Sierra Nevada; the Great Salt Lake; the western plains; Chicago; and the arrival in New York City—the bridges, Statue of Liberty, the city skyline seemed awesome to me at the age of nearly sixteen. During the three days' wait to board the SS *Vulcania* we toured ceaselessly from our Commodore Hotel room on 42d Street to museums, monuments, tops of skyscrapers.

But on our eventual return to San Francisco, it was my memories of The Stan Kenton Orchestra's live performances every evening in the hotel's grand parlor that garnered the most interest among my musician pals. Of course, Kenton's orchestra's performance held little interest for my parents, but to my musical buddies it was the only possible reason to go to New York City. I had to relate all of Kenton's soloists' performances and June Christy's captivating vocals to them.

At 11 o'clock in the morning of the appointed day of departure, my parents and I boarded the ship, stowed our luggage in the cabin, and proceeded to the huge dining hall to relax, admire the décor, and wait to order lunch. Within minutes a ship's officer arrived to deliver a cablegram to my father: "*Santa Lucia* encountered hurricane in Gulf of Mexico, suffered damage, rescued by U.S. Navy from Guantanamo Bay base. Ship being repaired in Navy shipyard. Please advise. Captain Terry."

14. All Aboard!

We were stunned. We never ordered lunch.

Returning to our cabin, we gathered our luggage, left the ship, and proceeded downtown to the Pan American travel office across the street from the Commodore Hotel. Finally, at the head of the line, dad requested three tickets for all of us to fly to Guantanamo. The clerk informed dad that it was a U.S. Naval Base with no facilities or lodging for civilians but that he could proceed under the circumstances with one ticket and be housed at the guest barracks to conduct his affairs.

The three of us returned to the SS *Vulcania,* which was scheduled to depart in a few hours. We repacked the luggage to one suitcase of dad's clothing and necessities, hugged and kissed him goodbye and wished him good luck, and did not see him again for three months.

Naturally, my parents' Italian families had all been aware of our trip for some time. Several planned to be at the Genoa dock to meet us on our arrival. What had happened; how long would it take for my father to get the ship back in running order; when would it proceed on its trip to Genoa—what were we to tell the folks waiting for us in Genoa? My mother and I were speechless. We could not react to the sudden shock of this terrible turn of events. Mother especially was in a terrible state and wondered what to tell the passengers who witnessed our being seated for lunch in the SS

Vulcania, departing hurriedly, only to return and dad darting back off the ship. We were no doubt the subject of considerable speculation. Mom had a lot of explaining to do, which did not make her any happier.

Mom and me on the SS *Vulcania*

The ship departed on time that evening and took a few days to get through the Gulf Stream's rough seas. The ocean finally settled down on Christmas evening. Learning that mom was a pianist, she was persuaded to play a few tunes, and I was talked into accompanying her on my trumpet for many of them. Yes, my parents insisted that I bring along my trumpet because they wished to show off my musical skills as well as mom's. But dad was in Cuba and what he was going through would be a total mystery to my mother and me for months.

The trip was no fun. The ship did remain a day or so in Naples to allow passengers to visit Pompeii; we were anxious to do so and witnessed the evidence of that final calamity of the ancient city. Oddly enough, spending almost a whole day viewing the remains of Pompeii and the museum there that is dedicated to preserving and displaying its human victims in their horrifying and instantaneous death throes put our personal anxieties in great perspective. And it also reminded me at the time of Mr. Tibbets, my high-school chemistry and geology teacher's dictum, delivered in his gravelly voice: "And gentlemen, remember there is no such thing as an extinct volcano."

In late December the SS *Vulcania* finally docked in Genoa and my mother and I were immediately greeted by many of my father's family members, whose first words in Italian were, "Where is Nino; what happened; when will he arrive?" We had few answers, but my mother was on the spot and tried to answer in a manner to allay their fears. Mom and I proceeded by train the next day to Turin to essentially move into my father's sister Maria's apartment with her young son, Sandro, and my father's mother, my elderly and beautiful grandmother, Lucia.

I slept in Sandro's small bedroom and the ladies managed somehow for many weeks. I quickly learned basic verbal Italian and passed the days studying my high-school textbooks, practicing my trumpet occasionally, and, after seeing to the repair of Aunt Maria's bike, I took to killing time, biking all over Turin when it was not snowing and the roads were reasonably clear. One day, close to my birthday in late February 1949, "Nonna" (my grandmother) Lucia asked me, "What would you like me to knit for your 17th birthday?" I quickly thought of a ski sweater: wool, turtleneck, gold/yellow body with double V's in dark blue (my high-school colors) on the front from the shoulders down to the belt buckle. My mother bought the yarn and we watched Nonna, who knitted like a machine while talking, conversing, and relating childhood stories, in less than three days complete the beautiful ski sweater I wore often on skiing trips and still treasure.

In early March my mother received a cablegram from dad advising of his arrival at the Rome airport —date, time, flight number. Mom was thrilled, so she and I took a train from Turin to Rome a day ahead of time; no dad and no explanation in the mail either. The trip back to Turin was woeful and I had to put on a brave face, console her, not to worsen her feelings, and again, we had nothing to explain to the family. Finally, in late March 1949 another cablegram: Stay put, will arrive at bus station in Turin at such-and-such date and time. Mom, Zia Maria, and I went to the bus station and dad showed up, looking terrible and saying little, low spirited but very happy to finally join us.

Me, many years later, wearing "The Sweater," with my wife, Sandra Paredi

The American Legacy of an Italian Motorcyclist

15. The Story

During the next few days dad proceeded to tell mom and me, Zia Maria, and his mother (Nonna Lucia) the following account of his three-month project in Guantanamo, Cuba. After checking in at the U.S. Naval Base he was assigned a room in the guest quarters and went immediately to the Base Hospital, where Captain Terry was still recovering from his ordeal. Terry was well attended and told dad exactly what had happened on the *Santa Lucia*. Before encountering the hurricane a few hundred miles west of Guantanamo in the Gulf of Mexico, the First and Second Mates assaulted Captain Terry and locked him in his cabin; in that confrontation there was a struggle, which resulted in Terry's broken arm. The two assailants were the senior members of the six-man crew recruited, interviewed, and hired in San Francisco by dad and Terry before the *Santa Lucia* embarked for Genoa.

The American Legacy of an Italian Motorcyclist

In the two days following the mutiny and Captain Terry's confinement, he learned that the two Mates had planned the mutiny to occur after the ship had entered the Atlantic Ocean. They would then take control and sail it to Oslo, Norway, where they would sell it. It was clear to Terry that he was a threat to their plan, and he would never see Norway, let alone Genoa. It would be reported in Norway that the Captain had fallen ill, died, and been buried at sea. The other members of the crew would also benefit somehow from the sale.

Nature intervened and provided a hurricane from which the *Santa Lucia* suffered: fortunately, within SOS hailing distance of the Guantanamo U.S. Naval Base at the eastern end of Cuba. The heavy seas for a day or two constantly over-washed the decks and descended to the ship's bilge, where its bilge pumps should have properly functioned to return the seawater overboard. Fortunately for Captain Terry, on the seawater's way to the bilge it carried too much coke, which ultimately choked the bilge pumps. The pumps failed, the ship foundered, and the First Mate was forced to send the SOS signal, which was received at the nearby U.S. Guantanamo Naval Base; a rescue vessel found and hauled the *Santa Lucia* to the naval port.

Captain Terry charged the two mutineers with their crimes; they were jailed in the base brig and Terry sent the news to my father, who was sitting down for lunch with mom and me on the SS *Vulcania*. After his interview with Captain Terry, dad set about the plan to have the shipyard clean the vessel up, repair or replace the bilge pumps, and restore the *Santa Lucia* to seaworthiness. He paid the repair bills from the $30,000 cash he had on consignment from members of San Francisco's Italian community for their family relatives in Italy. He was not worried at this point because the sale of the *Santa Lucia* in Genoa was to be worth millions and easily cover the *Santa Lucia*'s repair bill and replace those "consignments."

Within two weeks of the planned departure of the *Santa Lucia* from Guantanamo to Genoa, one of the partners in the group that financed the purchase of the ship appeared unannounced. Renzo Turco, the lawyer-partner from San Francisco, told my father that the remainder of the partners were concerned about the ship's situation in Guantanamo and had dispatched Renzo to check up on things and report back to them. A week later, dad was having breakfast in the mess hall and reading the local Spanish language newspaper. He was shocked to find a small article in Spanish reporting that the *Santa Lucia* had been sold by its San Francisco owners to a Senior Babun of a banana exporting company in Costa Rica.

Dad suddenly realized what Renzo had been doing in the short time he was there. He abandoned his breakfast and dashed up to the guest barracks to find Renzo packing his suitcase. Dad confronted Renzo with the newspaper article, demanding an explanation. Renzo responded by stating the partners had become concerned that the repair was taking so long. They were getting worried about the viability of the venture and had given Renzo a "power of attorney" to liquidate the ship if he so decided. My father resignedly accepted the conclusion of the project but demanded reimbursement of the cash that was not his that he used to pay the repair bill to the U.S. Navy. That was that. Dad prepared immediately to leave Guantanamo for Turin, Italy.

It was hardly "nothing ventured, nothing gained"; it was a bitter pill for dad and all of us to accept since he had worked so hard on the "cinch" for what turned out to be his last opportunity in his life to attain the "American Dream" of great success in the New World. What followed for two weeks were many road trips to visit his family all over Piedmonte, other than Turin, where my mother and I had felt that we must have outworn our welcome. That's when I first met my paternal grandfather, Ercole, and my father's other sister, Franca, her husband, Carlo, their daughter, Silvia, and the mysterious Maso, and saw the remains of the actual hole in the ground where Maso was hidden during daylight hours for many months, or years, to escape a much worse fate after his arduous solo trek from Ethiopia to Boves. In early April, 1949, dad, mom, and I finally returned by boat and railroad to San Francisco to our lives and expectations of "pre-great opportunity" times.

Clockwise: Lucia and Ercole Paredi; my father, Nino; and Maso

Maso's wife, their daughter Luisianna, Sandro, Maria, Maso

Once again, my father accompanied me to meet the
high school principal who had allowed me a brief
extension of what was to have been a Christmas

break. He accepted dad's explanation for my extended absence, but informed us that my return in the middle of April, the spring semester, meant there was no way the school system could give me credit for missing half of the semester of "civics," which was considered essential to graduate from high school in California. Worse yet, the civics course was only available in my high school in *next* year's spring semester, 1950. Ergo, I would have to concoct 1-1/2 years of unrequired electives to wait for the 1950 spring semester civics course. Could I complain after what dad had endured?

My father's next visit that day was to the office of two of the remaining financing partners of the *Santa Lucia* adventure. These two gentlemen shared an office and as soon as dad entered their office, unannounced, they jumped up and ran to him saying, "Hey, John, welcome back, tell us how the sale went, we're dying to hear all about it!"

Say *what*? That's right! Renzo had managed the rip-off of the year. There never was any "power of attorney." The partners, including Terry, immediately met to determine what legal options they had to resolve the problem with Mr. Turco.

The only legal option available would have been for the partners, who had lost their investments—or time, in dad's case—to hire an international maritime law attorney to pursue a lawsuit that could last years and incur unknown but

163

substantial expense. The consensus: not worth the time, trouble, and money.

Luckily, my father was able to return to his Civil Service Inspector of Naval Materials position; mom returned to her City of Paris millinery work; I got a summer job as a draftsman at a construction company and waited for the 1949-1950 extra semesters to satisfy California's requirement for high school graduation.

In retrospect, the *Santa Lucia* adventure had a very lucky outcome for me in a profession I knew nothing about at that time: a beautiful wife and two daughters—a life I could never have imagined or predicted.

16. My University Years

Dad was welcomed back to work as a full-time Inspector of Naval Materials. The post-WWII years kept the U.S. Navy very busy, as other U.S. governmental entities, reorganizing for a mostly reformed world. Mom's full-time job at the San Francisco City of Paris high-end department store's millinery shop continued, and I completed my extra fifth year in high school to satisfy the state-required civics course to graduate in the spring of 1950. I had anticipated graduating the prior year, as I was the student-body president then, but my extended and unplanned absence of three months during that spring semester provided me with an unanticipated different kind of education in Italy. I made the most of my extra year in high school, enrolling in numerous geology and other earth science-oriented courses that were well over and above those required to graduate.

The American Legacy of an Italian Motorcyclist

I was accepted at the University of California, Berkeley, in the fall of 1950, majoring in chemistry. I commuted from San Francisco my freshman year, starting at 6 o'clock every morning by public transportation to Berkeley to begin classes at 8 a.m. Chemistry majors were required to take a minimum one year of German language courses, eight total units. Taking an unrequired swimming course at 8 added another burden to my daily schedule; but I felt it necessary to make up for my inability to learn how to swim due to the polio epidemic of the early 1940s. Somehow, I got A's in German but B's in chemistry. This prompted my upper-class advisor to suggest that I change my major.

University of California-Berkeley, 1950s view

16. My University Years

The second semester I carpooled with a few other students to Berkeley, and one of them was about to graduate with a degree in petroleum engineering (PE). As soon as my car-pooling companion finished describing PE, I was sold on changing my major to PE. Its emphasis on earth sciences, which I had grown to love during my exposure to the field during my extra high school year, made a hit with me. For the next five years my summers were filled with part-time employment and college years of hard study, lots of fraternity fun, and spring breaks occupied with geology field trips on weekends. My week-long spring breaks were devoted to surface geology trips in the East Bay mountains and southern California oil basin while other college kids were at the beaches.

During those years, cash was the coin of the realm. There were no checking accounts, no credit cards. We did invest in Victory Bonds during WWII. Banks were only relied on for mortgages. I never had an allowance as a young kid, but I worked all the time: even during Christmas holiday breaks I would find temporary post office delivery jobs or work in department store clothing sales sections.

I was really fortunate during the three-month summer breaks during my university years when I had a flawless driving record to be hired as a delivery truck driver for the Railway Express Agency. At the end of WWII, my Uncle Johnny, who was married to mom's younger sister Olga, had returned safely from his Army Air Force assignment as a Glider Crew Chief for five years. Johnny found a long career with the Railway Express Agency and by the time that I was a university student Johnny was a district office manager at the South San Francisco branch. He was able to hire me every summer for five years to drive a large delivery truck, filling in for every one of his agency's regular truck drivers while they took their summer holidays. I would have sufficient money to pay for my entertainment, dates, etc., but I would give most of my earnings to my parents when I made good wages and, when I didn't, dad would always give me what I needed for the movies and dates, and the use of the family car was always available.

My trumpet performances with small trios or swing bands would yield minor income throughout high school and less during my college years. Upon graduating, I packed up the trumpet and forgot about it until several years after I retired, but happily picked it up again instead of playing golf. I started golf too late and never had time enough to practice and improve; tennis was my favorite athletic pursuit.

The University of California is a "land grant" institution, thereby being required by the federal government to provide freshman and sophomore male students with *mandatory* military science courses, two units per semester, and *voluntary* courses in military sciences in their sophomore and senior years. Those students who are interested in graduating with a military commission as second lieutenants in any one of the U.S. armed forces reserves may apply to be selected when graduating with a degree in any field. The program is called the Reserve Officers Training Corps (ROTC).

In 1950, the Korean War required drafting of men to fulfill the needs of the armed services for the duration of that war. It therefore became very popular for young men of draft age attending land-grant colleges and universities to apply for admission to "upper division" ROTC. If accepted to the program, based upon grade-point levels during their freshman and sophomore years, they would be assured of completing their studies in their chosen field and would graduate with a commission in the armed services.

Several other members of my Phi Kappa Psi fraternity qualified for the ROTC program; a few others either did not qualify or chose to avoid the opportunity and were drafted into service at entry ranks for the duration of the war. I attained my reserve officer's commission in 1954 and was allowed to continue my studies at U.C.-Berkeley until I received my Bachelor of Sciences degree in petroleum engineering in June 1955. My Italian visit in 1949, the changing of my major from chemistry to petroleum engineering, and the hours spent in military sciences and German all contributed to me getting my "PE" degree a year later than planned, but I had also skipped the second grade in elementary school and considered that I broke even, time-wise!

After one year of commuting from home to Berkeley, I ran the numbers to find that it would be less expensive to consider joining a fraternity rather than continuing wasting three hours daily carpooling or taking public transportation. Changing my major from chemistry to petroleum engineering also required a significant number of subjects entailing lab work and geology field trips, sometimes on weekends, which would further compound commuting problems.

My parents understood, so I joined one of the "Greek letter" fraternities of the 40 located adjacent the U.C.-Berkeley campus: Phi Kappa Psi, one of the many nationwide such organizations. There were 17 of us newly accepted members, called "pledges," in the frat house of about 40 members. Some of the upperclassmen were WWII veterans completing their GI Bill-supported educations. There were serious guidelines established by the upperclassmen regarding study hours and grades. But there were also serious parties during the semesters in our chapter house prior to major football weekends, homecoming events, and any other excuse to have a party.

16. My University Years

One such event in 1952 when I was an officer of the chapter was the annual homecoming weekend, when every one of the other far-flung campuses of the University of California was invited to attend homecoming week at the "mother" campus. A major annual football contest in the Berkeley campus football stadium, normally against the Stanford University team on Saturday, would be played after a lengthy homecoming parade. The parade always featured floats sponsored by the Greek-letter fraternities, sororities, and other U.C.-Berkeley student organizations.

Weeks prior to that year's homecoming weekend event, a group of us met in our frat house to determine what kind of a float we would enter. The landmark element of the U.C.-Berkeley campus is the handsome campanile clock tower at the center of the campus, visible from all points of the compass in the Bay Area. Its official name is Sather Tower, after an early wealthy benefactor, Jane Sather. The campanile is 307 feet tall, the third highest in the world, with a 61-bell carillon. It is modeled after the tower in Venice, Italy, in the Piazza San Marco.

One of our brothers on the float committee in the chapter house had a bright idea: His family owned and operated a concrete factory in the nearby east bay town of Walnut Creek, which had a forklift that we could borrow. We could build a 25-foot-tall replica of Sather Tower on the forklift at ground level upon the fork. The operator and scion of the factory, Jay Forni, would maneuver the forklift on a zig-zag course from the start of the parade to its end while carefully raising and lowering the campanile on its fork to avoid colliding with the occasional overhead electrical cables.

We jumped on the idea with alacrity. It was brilliant. In the two weeks prior to the event we had the forklift in the parking lot behind our frat house and constructed a replica of the tower, complete with a heavy bronze bell "borrowed" from a San Francisco cable car, installing the bell within the tower top. Jay operated the forklift and Warren Hellman, both of them our Gamma Chapter brothers of Phi Kappa Psi, were well practiced in the float's and bell's operation. The parade was attended by thousands of students, the public, and members of the local press and followed by the football game and a serious party in our social hall (read "bar") in our frat-house basement.

The following morning our house telephone rang incessantly with calls from concerned and outraged parents demanding to know who in the world was responsible for entering the "obscene" float in the homecoming parade, which scandal made front-page news in every newspaper in the Bay Area. None of us were aware that someone had attached a poster at the base of the campanile on the forklift reading "SATHERS LAST ERECTION." No one in our house admitted to having been guilty to the poster fiasco and someone came up with the suspicion that the Beta Theta Pi members of our next-door neighbor's frat house were the culprits. That suspicion was not accepted by the U.C. Student Council or other U.C. authorities, and our chapter was placed on one semester's social probation and forbidden to conduct any social activities in our house for six months. We found remedies to continue some social functions at commercial facilities in Oakland and blamed our neighbors when confronted by our parents.

Primo, my maternal grandfather, was the missing person in my life. I heard stories about him but never saw or met him. Until lately, I had never even seen a photo of him. In all the photos that include him, his image has been carefully scrubbed out with black pencil shading. It wasn't until recently that I studiously examined several black and white photo prints in my family albums to discover mom's deliberate tampering. One of these photos shows family groupings in Italy with his visage carefully obliterated. Only then did I appreciate the extent of her dislike of him. I had no idea what Primo looked like until recently. I phoned both of my cousins in California to ask if either of them might have a photo with his image. Sure enough, Nancy, one of the two daughters of mom's younger sister, my Aunt Olga, said, "Sure, I have one, and it's the only one, so I'll mail it to you but please mail it back when you're finished with it." My cousin Nancy added that Primo was tall and handsome, but his seated position in the only photo that exists of him gives little hint of his height. Nancy's mother, Olga, must have told her about his height.

On a couple of occasions in my youth, dad casually mentioned to me that Primo had phoned him to request that he come down to the local jail to bail him out. These calls occurred long after "prohibition" laws were repealed. Not only that, but the belief was that all communications between Primo and his prior family, including my father—Primo's only son-in-law—were discontinued. My father had refused the job offer Primo made him on his arrival with my mother from Italy in 1929. Primo apparently continued his bootlegging enterprise but was evading paying federal taxes on his product, which he continued to distill in the Oakland hills. The odd thing is that my dad was the only person who Primo knew he could rely upon to bail him out, and that dad felt obliged to do it more than once.

Fair to say, I was always curious about Primo, but understood why he was considered bad news before and after his divorce from Asunta. In my second year at U.C.-Berkeley I avoided the tedious, expensive, and impractical commuting back and forth from San Francisco by joining a fraternity across the street from the campus. I often spent the weekends at home with my parents. One

16. My University Years

Sunday night they drove and dropped me off at my frat house. No sooner had they returned home that my father got a call from Primo. It was not to ask him to come and bail him out. It was to determine whether I would be amenable to meet him sometime in Oakland. Dad called me immediately. I was certainly surprised, but thought about it for a moment and told dad, "Why not," unenthusiastically. My dad said, "Okay, I'll pass that along to Primo." Our meeting never happened, but I was not surprised. Dad and I never mentioned it again and dad never heard from Primo again. Dad never pursued the curious invitation either. It is fair to conjecture that whoever might have been Primo's wife or partner at the time got wind of his idea and gave him her opinion of it.

Clockwise: Primo, Asunta, Erma, and Eda

17. Welcome to the Army

My parents proudly attended my U.S. Army commissioning ceremony at the University of California Memorial Stadium in Berkeley, June 1954. Major General William Dean presided at the ceremony welcoming the young lieutenants to the U.S. Army as newly commissioned officers. General Dean was the highest ranking general ever to have been captured by the enemy and had spent three years held by the North Korean Army. He was a graduate of U.C.-Berkeley and received the highest awards and recognition from the U.S. government upon his release for leading the 24th Infantry Division, and was awarded the Medal of Honor for his actions on July 20 and 21, 1950, during the Battle of Taejon in South Korea.

I was particularly pleased that my parents attended the ceremony because I was ordered to active duty after I graduated in June 1955 with a

B.S. in Petroleum Engineering, but before the Class of 1955 graduation ceremony was held.

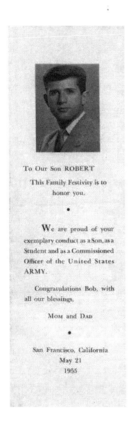

To Our Son ROBERT

This Family Festivity is to honor you.

•

We are proud of your exemplary conduct as a Son, as a Student and as a Commissioned Officer of the United States ARMY.

Congratulations Bob, with all our blessings.

MOM and DAD

•

San Francisco, California
May 21
1955

FIOR d'ITALIA
SAN FRANCISCO

MENU

COCKTAIL
•
HORS D'OEUVRES
•
TOSSED GREEN SALAD
•
MINESTRINA REALE
•
ROAST PRIME RIBS OF BEEF
BAKED POTATOES
•
JUMBO SQUAB CASSEROLE
WILD RICE STUFFING
•
ASPARAGI ALLA MILANESE
•
ASSORTED CHEESE
•
FRESH FRUIT
•
GATEAU ST. HONOREE
ICE CREAM
•
DEMI TASSE
•
VIN BLANC – VIN ROUGE – CHAMPAGNE
LIQUEUR

Program and menu from my parents' celebratory dinner honoring me upon my commissioning into the Army Corps of Engineers

178

17. Welcome to the Army

My mother and me at my commissioning

The American Legacy of an Italian Motorcyclist

I was ordered to report to Fort Belvoir, Alexandria, Virginia, for three months of intensive training in the arts and sciences of military engineering. My training ranged from blowing up and building bridges, deploying and clearing minefields, detecting and disarming booby traps, building roads and airfields, map reading, marksmanship, and heavy equipment operations. Every two weeks a group of 90 newly commissioned second lieutenants arrived at Fort Belvoir, the home base of the Army Engineer Corps.

At one point in the program each student was required to develop and present a mock training lesson on a topic of his choice to the whole class; I picked map reading and developed a lesson plan and presented the lesson. While monitoring all the mock teaching classes, the staff must have graded me well enough for me to be considered a candidate to remain as part of the faculty at Fort Belvoir. At the beginning of our last two weeks there, each of us was given a four-page form to complete. We were advised that the completed questionnaire would determine the posts where we would be stationed for the remainder of our duty. Before receiving the form, I was privately notified that I need not complete it if I wished to remain at Fort Belvoir to become an instructor to incoming classes for the next 21 months. The job offer to remain as part of the faculty was welcome, but I respectfully declined it. I desperately wanted an

17. Welcome to the Army

assignment anywhere in Europe with any kind of an "MOS" (military occupational specialty), even if it meant as a combat engineering platoon leader.

I took the questionnaire back to my apartment that evening and proceeded to fill it out. On page #2 I even entered the code-number for "combat platoon leader" to increase my chances of a European assignment. Turning to the top half of page #3 I was surprised to find "Foreign Language Proficiency." A matrix of four lines and four columns led me to eagerly enter Italian, French, German, and Speak, Read, Write: "Yes, Yes, Yes" on every space.

Three days later I was informed that I had been assigned to Bordeaux, France, as the Assistant Operations Officer for the 83d Reinforced Engineering Construction Battalion. Of my apartment mates, two got European duty, one got U.S. duty, and two got Pacific Theater duty. I was elated, and immediately phoned my parents: I was coming home to San Francisco on a one-week leave; I would return to New York to board a Navy ship to sail to Hamburg, then proceed by train to Bordeaux; and please locate my French language textbook last seen and used six years ago.

It was a bittersweet and temporary homecoming, visiting all the family and friends and preparing for another unfamiliar destination. It would be my second trip to Europe. My parents were thrilled and immediately started talking about visiting me as soon as I settled in Bordeaux; they planned to continue to Italy, and, with me, visit dad's family in Milan, Turin, and Boves. Letters had been flowing back and forth freely since the war's end between dad's family in Italy and San Francisco. My father's family in Italy was prospering once again after all the trauma endured during the war that had concluded 10 years prior.

I arrived in Bordeaux in early September 1955 and temporarily settled in the Hotel Bordeaux. Camp Bussac was the NATO base 40 kilometers north of Bordeaux where numerous U.S. Army battalions, including the 83d Reinforced Engineering Battalion, were headquartered with two of its five companies; three other companies were stationed within one- to two-hour drives from the headquarters. A U.S. Army bus provided daily transport between Bordeaux and Camp Bussac.

The day after my arrival in Bordeaux I made it to Bussac and reported to the 83d Battalion HQ at 11 a.m., the two-desk office of its commander, a lieutenant colonel and his adjutant, a major. I strode into their office and, at attention, announced myself to Major X., who had my personnel file open on his desk. Returning my salute, he said, "Well, Lt. Paredi, we've been looking forward to your arrival for some time now because we can't even order a bottle of wine here in a French restaurant and we understand you speak fluent French!" *That was a real relief,* I thought, and I immediately responded "Yessir!" while actually thinking, *Well, not really, and I quit studying French in high school six years ago.* A few minutes of pleasantries passed with the Commander of the 83d at the nearby desk pretending to be studying some papers. I began thinking, *Am I lucky or what? Here I am in the land of the blind and I am the one-eyed King!*

After several more minutes of pleasantries, Major X. announced that I was the new assistant to Captain Z., the Battalion Operations Officer, and called him to come and meet me. Captain Z. promptly appeared and, after greetings, offered the following: "You know, why don't we all go to the officers mess for lunch now and come back to the conference room so that Lt. Paredi can call up Capitaine L. in Bordeaux to arrange our overdue meeting with him and his staff to review the agenda; we can review it with Lt. Paredi after lunch to make sure the French are ready to address these issues which must be resolved."

What a wonderful idea! They all agreed to pursue it after lunch.

I lost my appetite, but I had no choice but to face the music or the firing squad after being sent to Germany, after all. On return to the small conference room, five of them gathered and I was handed the telephone, Capitaine L.'s phone

183

number, and the agenda items for next week's meeting in Bordeaux. All of our construction projects in the area had to be constantly communicated to our allies for many reasons. I did have the blessed advantage of having the *only* telephone in the room: no loudspeakers other than the one in the phone's handset glued to my ear. A gracious and understanding French "officer and a gentleman" was on the other end of the line who probably could speak better English than I could speak French.

After my salutation to the French officer, things went very smoothly because he would slowly repeat everything I said in perfect French with more details, and most of the time I would simply say, "Oui, oui, c'est ca" (meaning "Yes, yes, that's right") or "Pas exactement" (meaning "not exactly") and the good Capitaine would embellish or correct my French and we would be back to "Oui, oui, c'est ca." I spent much more time the following week with my French language textbook than I had on the way over; and I continued to play "the King."

The following week the joint meeting in Bordeaux took place with few language problems. Before the conclusion of that first introductory meeting at the Battalion HQ, Major X. apologized that I would have to arrange my own living arrangement "off-post" because the bachelor officers quarters (BOQ) at Camp Bussac were all assigned but I would receive a $20/day off-post living allowance.

17. Welcome to the Army

And Major X. finally had a fatherly bit of advice regarding my choice of a personal automobile: "We hope you don't decide to purchase a high-powered sports car because we have lost too many young officers to car accidents here." Within a few weeks living at the Hotel Bordeaux, I met another young lieutenant in the 83d living in the hotel also being paid $20/day due to the BOQ shortage at the base, Lt. George Harris. George had bought a second-hand Jaguar 140-modified and we immediately became close friends.

I had figured out by then that I could get away with ignoring the good Major X.'s fatherly advice and had purchased a brand-new, ice-blue Austin-Healey 100, two-seat convertible.

Me and the Austin-Healey

The American Legacy of an Italian Motorcyclist

George and I quickly found rental quarters at a local French farmhouse midway between Camp Bussac and Bordeaux. We had one-half of the two-story home at the farm/vineyard home of a middle-aged couple, the Blandas, who managed the local baron and baroness's extensive property. George and I, pooling our resources, easily handled renting the half-house, which had been remodeled by two prior American GI families. Happily, they had upgraded the second-floor bathroom of the two-bedroom half-house to conform to American standards.

We were treated as part of our landlord's family since their two sons were working in Paris. George and I paid the landlords infinitely more than their previous tenants—German officers—had paid them, which was precisely nothing!

My parents made good on their promise to meet with me in Paris during my first year in Bordeaux. I drove to Paris in my Austin-Healey to meet them. It was a beautiful morning, and I drove through vineyards and villages, and past the ornate cathedral at Chartres. I met dad and mom, and proceeded to Italy to meet again with dad's family, which now included two of his nieces. Silvia Monteverde was dad's sister Franca Monteverde's daughter and Luisanna was dad's brother Maso's daughter, both of them striking young ladies. By this time, dad's sister Maria's son, Sandro, was becoming a chef in Turin. My father took great pride re-introducing me as an officer in the U.S. Army.

Mom and dad on top of the Duomo, Milano

The American Legacy of an Italian Motorcyclist

Sandro, Aunt Maria, me, my mother, 1957

In the spring of 1956, my housemate was ordered for two weeks' temporary duty to Germany. Since George's bedroom would be vacant for that period, I thought to invite my Aunt Maria from Turin to visit me and be shown about since I would be on duty. Maria was fluent in French but had never left Italy in her life. She had housed me and my mom for three months in Turin in 1949 while dad had been in Cuba tending to his *Santa Lucia* ship venture crisis.

I proposed the idea to Madame Blanda, who heartily approved. I wrote an invitation to Maria, who excitedly accepted. Maria arrived at the

17. Welcome to the Army

Bordeaux rail station as scheduled. I fetched her "home," and introduced her to Madame Blanda. The two of them, of similar age, got along like schoolgirls for the weeks while I attended to duty. The visit also served as another improvement to my French fluency, even though George and I had often been dating young French ladies.

The family environment of Maria's visit and her warm welcome from Madame Blanda was much less formal and provided more laughs for us. Maria wrote dad, in San Francisco, about her experience in France, which added to family bonds that had been curtailed during the not-so-distant WWII.

Over the years, I came to realize that Aunt Maria's little boy, Sandro, was certainly born "out of wedlock." Maybe my father on his first trip returning to Italy after WWII might have been informed by someone in the family who the boy's father was. Had he been informed of exactly who it was, other than a German military man, he might have said that Sandro was the son of Maria's Italian fiancé, or her Italian husband, or an Italian soldier who was killed. But, if my dad had learned the true answer was a German male, the less said about it by anyone in her family, the better. The most likely supposition of the truth being the latter probably was the truth. No one, possibly save Sandro, ever knew the whole truth. And anyone else's belief would be a supposition. Sandro did become a restaurant chef but disappeared from the family news as far as I know. During Maria's two-week visit with me in the Bordeaux area while I was in the Army I never dared ask her how he was and she never brought it up. So, I supposed Sandro's father was a German!

Aunt Maria and Sandro, 1957

Included in my duties as the assistant battalion operations officer were quarterly plans for "NODEX" exercises conducted by the battalion. The Bordeaux marine port facilities were

17. Welcome to the Army

determined to be a critical asset in the event of a missile air attack by Russian forces to destroy those facilities. The port was inland and far upstream on the Gironde River. One particular exercise was conducted off the riverbank at a small village in the Bordeaux wine country 30 kilometers north of the Bordeaux port. The exercise consisted of many elements, starting with large marine barges anchored to the river bottom 100 meters offshore connected to the road on the riverbank with a series of floating inflatable pontoon rafts that supported a bridgeway from the road to the two connected barges.

Supply vessels carrying military equipment and NATO troops would arrive from the south Atlantic to moor adjacent to the barges to offload their cargo, which would be transferred to the shore over the floating roadway or transported to the far bank of the river by an aerial tramway erected from the barges to the eastern bank of the river. All of the floating part of the system had to be anchored in the river upstream and downstream to resist the river current, which would reverse directions every six to seven hours.

The construction of the systems required three weeks of intensive activity followed by several weeks of actual operation, including supply ships arrivals, offloading of troops and equipment being transported to the near and far shores of the river by the pontoon floating roadway or aerial trams suspended by cables to the far shore. The near-shore of the river was in full view of the village's inhabitants and its older citizens had the unrestrained view of the frenetic daytime activities from the bar and restaurants' patrons all day long along the river-front. It was quite a show for the villagers. Of particular merriment to the patrons was the spectacle one afternoon of one of our "D-8" large "caterpillar" bulldozers sinking out of sight into the exposed mud-flat at low tide. The "cat" helped locate one of several one-cubic-meter concrete anchors, of several required, to secure support cables to hold the barges against the up- and downstream forces of the shifting river currents during the entire exercise. The good news was that no battalion personnel were lost or suffered injuries through the entire six-week exercise and that the village's citizens were provided much free entertainment throughout the event.

My father had put his *Santa Lucia* business fiasco behind him, never looked back, and was still enjoying his position as a Civilian Naval Inspector in San Francisco. I described my U.S. Army duties in the Bordeaux area to dad, which fascinated him. My activities in France were much more of a "civil" engineering nature, which dad could identify with, rather than "petroleum" engineering.

I was already thinking about my post-military career once I left my Army assignment. Dad and I

192

were then establishing a new kind of adult relationship based upon a mutual respect for one another's ambitions at different stages of our lives. My plans were very fluid regarding still-forming ideas of what I was thinking about doing after leaving the Army. I promised my Italian relatives that I'd meet with them again before returning to the U.S. in the coming year. George's and my lives proceeded apace as a result of our growing command of French, our lifestyles unencumbered by having to live at the Bussac BOQ, and our sports cars.

My car, being new, was very reliable; George's, previously part of Prince Sihanouk's automobile stable, was not. The "Jag" was often in repair mode, so it was well that we were roommates at the farmhouse. The seasons were pronouncedly variable, from light snowy winters to beautiful summers. We prepared meals and fed ourselves with provisions purchased at the Bussac GI commissary, but were visited almost every evening at dinnertime by Madame Blanda, who was worried we might go hungry. Our kitchens were practically interconnected on the ground floor, which gave Madame unfettered access to our kitchen and dining room.

She was a wonderful woman and we were coddled as her sons would have been. As well as we fed ourselves, she would often insist we just "try" her guinea hen or "sample" rabbit or chicken dishes;

how could we resist politely without hurting her feelings? Consequently, we both put on close to 15 pounds during our residence there.

George was from the Midwest and a fan of corn on the cob, which was often available at the Bussac Camp Commissary. When George shopped and American "Golden Bantam" corn from the U.S. was available, the two of us would cook up at least six cobs of corn to accompany our dinner. On one such evening as we were munching down on our corncobs, Madame Blanda knocked on the dining room door, entered, and was aghast upon observing "the Americans" relishing corn on the cob. She about-faced and called her husband to come and observe the two savages consuming cattle and hog feed that would never be eaten by a Frenchman. Our explanation that the corn was imported from the U.S. and bore no resemblance to French or European "maize" fell on deaf ears as the Blandas laughingly shook their heads in disbelief. They politely declined our invitation to join us and just "try" it.

18. Gobsmacked!

Every lieutenant on the Bussac NATO base was
often required to serve as "Officer of the Day"
representing the commander of the base in his
absence. The working hours of most commissioned
personnel at the base were a nominal eight hours
per day. The OD would report to the Base
Commander, a colonel, at his office at 4 o'clock in
the afternoon. The lieutenant would receive the
assignment in person from the commander in his
office, be presented with his sidearm—a loaded 45-
caliber automatic pistol—and receive the
assignment with any specific instructions.

Colonel Barton was known to take pleasure in
making a young lieutenant's first assignment as
the OD as intimidating as possible. It was a no-
sleep, overnight duty involving answering
emergency calls and being driven in a jeep several
times around the perimeter of the huge camp to
make sure the perimeter guards were standing and

not sleeping. There were a few companies of Polish Army soldiers at the base whose sole duty was to deploy a trio of their soldiers at regular intervals along the fenced perimeter of the base at all hours to prevent entry to the base anywhere except the main gate, which was staffed permanently by armed guards 24 hours/day.

The only redeeming aspect of being the OD was checking in to the Base Commander's HQ office and being welcomed by his secretary/translator, a beautiful, red-headed young English woman, Miss Sheila Weevers. After a minute or two of pleasantries Miss Weevers would escort the OD to the commander's desk and depart. I performed the OD task at least once monthly.

In the spring of 1956, I received a call from Miss Weevers—now "Sheila"—inviting me and any companion to a party on Saturday night at such-and-so location in Bordeaux around 9 o'clock. I asked if I could bring along another lieutenant buddy of mine, Tom Patton: No problem. We showed up around 9:30 to an apartment crowded with a dozen or so couples, including a group of three couples that included Sheila and two other young ladies, all with their dates, all American officers from Camp Bussac.

Tom and I wandered over to introduce ourselves to Sheila and her companions. Upon Sheila's introduction of her younger sister Sandra, I was

18. Gobsmacked!

"gobsmacked," a curious Anglicism meaning *astounded, speechless, dumbstruck.* I had never seen such a beautiful young woman in my life. Tom and I mingled among the rest of guests for more introductions, got drinks, and wandered back near Sheila's group. Standing closer to Sheila's group, I happened to overhear one of the men suggest to the rest that they proceed to the nearby Merignac French Airfield Officers Club.

Drawing Tom aside, I suggested that we give Sheila's group a head start of 20 minutes or so, and then proceed to the Officers Club at Merignac, with which we were quite familiar. Tom and I arrived there as planned and took a couple of seats at the bar, ordered drinks, and glanced around the dance floor to see booths on the far side where Sheila and her friends were seated. I could not resist glancing continuously at Sandra in the group. After a half hour of this, Tom said, "When are you going to go over there and ask her to dance?" I replied, "As soon as I finish this drink." So it was that we danced. Sandra mentioned that she lived with her sister Sheila in Bordeaux while working as an *au pair* in the same building and attending the University of Bordeaux.

The following week I dropped by the sister's ground-floor apartment of a five-story apartment house, rang the bell and, after Sandra answered the bell and we exchanged pleasantries, I asked her for a date the following weekend: "Busy" was the discouraging reply. How about the following weekend? "Busy." How about the weekend after that? "Alright."

Within six months, Sandra and I were a couple, and I had to move to Bordeaux to a small apartment since my farm-mate's two-year term of duty was over. Sandra continued to live with her sister until Sheila, also having finished a private job of translating a medical treatise in French to English, decided to quit her job at Camp Bussac. Knowing that Sheila would be returning to England to her parent's home before my army tour was over, an idea came to me. I had a one-month leave coming and would be driving to northern Italy to say goodbye to my Italian relatives. I could add a solo trip to England to meet Sandra and Sheila's parents to "plead my case" regarding Sandra. Would Sheila prepare the ground for such a visit while Sandra remained in Bordeaux to complete her university and au-pair commitment?

The plan was set in motion. Sheila asked for a lift in my Austin-Healey to Nice, on my way to Italy, to spend some Mardi-Gras time with friends there on her way to London. I drove Sheila to Nice, spent a couple of days celebrating Mardi Gras with her friends, and then drove to Turin and Milan to visit aunts and cousins. I then drove solo nonstop for 22 hours, before the autostradas were built, arriving at my Bordeaux apartment at 7 in the morning to crash all day and night. With one week

18. Gobsmacked!

of leave left I drove the following morning to Paris, flew to London to meet Sandra's parents and many other relatives, with Sheila having arranged it all ahead of my arrival. On my way to drive to the Paris airport from Bordeaux, I left two parcels on the ground level window ledge of Sandra's now-solo apartment, having no time to even say hello.

Days before my departure from Milan to drive to Bordeaux, I was strolling through the Duomo de Milano Galleria complex with my cousin Silvia, who was about Sandra's age. I had already purchased a pretty Italian umbrella as a surprise gift for Sandra. Silvia and I passed an upscale woman's shoe shop in the Galleria and I mentioned to Silvia how Sandra loved Italian women's shoes. *What a great idea*, I thought as we entered the shop. The saleslady approached and I asked Silvia to pick out the most stunning pair of high-heeled beige leather shoes. The next obvious question was size. I had not a clue. The saleslady laughed; I sized up Silvia's height, body type, and feet and asked Silvia to try on a pair of shoes that fit her. I bought the nicely wrapped shoes, and took them and the umbrella back with me to Bordeaux. Those were the parcels I left on Sandra's window ledge three days later. The shoes were a perfect fit. Such was Cinderella's, my, and Sandra's luck.

Me with my cousin Silvia, Sandra's "foot-size" model

Sheila and her parents met me on my arrival in London and drove me to their residence in Gidea Park, Romford, Essex. During the following several days I was introduced to a large number of Sandra's local aunts, uncles, and cousins, as well

18. Gobsmacked!

as Sandra's younger sister and brother, Jacqueline and Peter. I learned that Sandra's mother, Catherine ("Cath"), was one of 14 children born into a Scottish family, while Sandra's father, Jack, was an only child and had served in the British Airforce during WWII. Most of Cath's siblings lived locally and were married with children. I was faced with such a profusion of Sandra's immediate relatives that I was overwhelmed comparing them to my own family's scant size back in San Francisco.

The hospitality I encountered while meeting all these relatives of Sandra's did put me at ease. Nonetheless, it also made me feel that I had plenty of people sizing me up and wondering if I was really the guy who deserved Sandra. I was beginning to wonder if the idea of meeting the whole Weevers "clan" was a good idea after all. Having said that, Cath, who had served me breakfast in bed every morning in "the crow's nest" bedroom on the third floor of their home, alleviated anxieties I had about being accepted by the "clan."

On the final full day of my visit, I asked Sheila to arrange a meal with just the four of us: Cath, her mother, Jack, her father, Sheila, and me. I wished to explain my situation regarding my actual and future employment and the academic and military credentials that I would be drawing upon after leaving the Army in six months. I wanted to make it plain that I would not wish to marry before I secured a good job in my field of petroleum engineering. That could take a few months and a year of employment before I might be qualified to return to England to marry Sandra. Sandra was in her final few months of residence in Bordeaux and the two of us would probably quit Bordeaux at the same time, with Sandra returning home and me likewise returning to San Francisco to start a job search. I and other engineering majors at U.C.-Berkeley had been interviewed at the beginning of our final year of study by a number of oil corporations. All the corporations that had interviewed me knew I had a two-year commitment to the U.S Army upon graduation. I was advised to "keep in touch with us when you are discharged three years from now, and good luck." That was the best that I could do.

On my return from London to Bordeaux from my intimidating one-week visit with Sandra's family, I gave her a rundown of my meetings with her family. I needed help remembering the names of all the aunts, uncles, cousins, and grandparents I had met. If Sandra ever got any feedback from her parents or sister Sheila who, no doubt, had prepared the schedule for my visit, she never passed it on and I never thought of asking or didn't dare ask. I had moved to Bordeaux several months before then and we only had about five more months together before my assignment would be over. I never did get on one knee to perform the traditional wedding proposal. We certainly spoke of marriage and were both committed to the idea and plan. It was a pretty daring scheme, since we had no idea how long it would take me to secure employment or where it would be. In retrospect, we surely took a lot for granted regarding our future together.

Two months prior to my scheduled release from duty in Bordeaux I had to turn my Austin-Healey in to the Transportation Corps, which was obliged to ship all officers' vehicles back to New York City, at government expense, to be retrieved by their owners at Fort Hamilton Maritime Facility. I received my transportation orders to report to Livorno, Italy, in late April to board a troopship bound for NYC.

Sandra and I decided to depart Bordeaux together to spend four days of April in Paris before we each would proceed to our homes separately: Gidea Park, Essex, for Sandra, and San Francisco, California, for me. It was a stressful parting for both of us, but I waved to Sandra at one of the Paris rail stations for London as we each committed to keep one another informed of our homecomings, in particular my progress in seeking employment. It was certainly an unforgettable "April in Paris" for us both.

The American Legacy of an Italian Motorcyclist

19. Homecomings

The trip to San Francisco for me started with a tedious uneventful troopship passage from Livorno, Italy, to New York harbor, with a joyful reunion between dad and me dockside at Fort Hamilton. As soon as Sandra and my plans to depart Bordeaux were settled, I invited dad to meet me on my arrival date in New York City, and there was dad waving and shouting with my Austin-Healey in the background among a score of vehicles awaiting their owners. The plan was for the two of us to remain at a hotel in NYC for a week, during which I was required to go through discharge processing. I spent 90 percent of the time there signing hundreds of discharge documents for Army servicemen awaiting their discharge. That took care of Monday through Friday, and in my spare time the two of us caught up with my friends, previously discharged but living in and around NYC. We got together every evening so they could meet my father and reminisce about their time with me in the service.

The day after that I was officially discharged, and dad and I embarked on a five-day road trip from New York City to San Francisco. Dad had flown from San Francisco to NYC to meet me and take turns driving several days later in my Austin-Healey 100 to San Francisco. Driving off from NYC the first day of our trip we soon entered the Pennsylvania Turnpike heading west, with no stoplights or intersections for a few hours that morning. It was the very first divided highway with no traffic lights or intersections from border to border of a state in the U.S. What a wonder; you only had to stop for fuel, restrooms, or a meal. There were such facilities at regular intervals the whole way and every one of them looked just like the last one: Howard Johnson's locations with all of the above including many choices of dishes and beverages. Many years later, the network of interstate federal highways started appearing with similar facilities. Dad would marvel, "Only in America." It didn't take too long before McDonald's and similar fast food competitors became common in many developed countries all over the world.

The 12-hour days of dad and me taking turns driving the Austin-Healey was an unbridled joy for both of us and came off like clockwork. At 5:30 in the afternoon we arrived at The City of Paris Department Store employees' exit door to greet my mother, who was finishing her regular week in the store's millinery shop. My parents and I had all this planned for weeks. I had done a round-trip drive between San Francisco and Atlantic City, New Jersey, with a couple of fraternity brothers five years before for our fraternity's annual convention. We had done that trip in three days and nights of nonstop driving for budgetary reasons, but this drive, most of it with the top down and dad taking turns driving, was so special, with so much to talk about, was unforgettable.

My immediate priority during those five days in New York City waiting for my discharge was to call the Standard Oil of New Jersey HQ Personnel Department to request an appointment. SONJ was one of the four corporations that interviewed me at U.C.-Berkeley before my graduation and military service. I explained my situation over the phone and was immediately granted an appointment. I told the representative at the interview that I was to be discharged that week and wished to apply for employment as a petroleum engineer with SONJ, and was given the necessary forms to prepare and return from San Francisco.

Soon after arriving home I contacted the other three corporations that had interviewed me, requesting similar job application material. I had the four job applications in process within three weeks of my return home. My mother was thrilled to have me home again and made calls to take me around to all the family members in the area and the banquets at Nonna's were organized. I had immediately telephoned Sandra and we compared our homecomings. For the next several weeks I was devoted to communicating with my high-priority prospective employers. I advertised the Austin-Healey for sale, caught up with old pals and fraternity brothers, and went on a few fishing trips in the High Sierras.

Within a month or so of applying to the top four corporations, job offers materialized from them all. I had made it clear in all my applications and interviews that I was available for domestic or foreign positions; two offers were for domestic U.S. employment and two were for foreign locations. Most importantly, I was not a freshly graduated, inexperienced candidate, but one with two years of experience with the U.S. Army Corps of Engineers in a responsible battalion command-staff position.

I wasted no time in reviewing the offers and decided to have a sit-down meeting with dad to seek his advice on the matter. I was sensitive to the fact that I had been matriculating for five years across the bay at U.C.-Berkeley and just completed two years of military service in France. The offers consisted of one in northern California, one in Texas, and two in Venezuela. My father and I sat down one afternoon to review the offers. He had but one question: "So, what's the problem?"

19. Homecomings

There was no problem at all, but I felt I needed dad's "buy-in" before accepting the top offer in Venezuela. Each of the foreign start-up salaries was almost 100% higher than the top domestic offers. In addition, both the Venezuelan ones included an immediate one month's annual vacation versus the domestic offers of two weeks of vacation after the first five years. The Venezuelan offers paid vacation travel to home of record (San Francisco). Most remarkably, the Venezuelan offers both provided two months' bonus salary, called *utilidades*, paid every December: 14 months' salary for 11 months of work. I looked at a map to find out where Lake Maracaibo was, and then telephoned Sandra to suggest wedding plans for late 1958.

The Austin-Healey sold quickly. I prepared a shipment of "bachelor" property, including records and turntable and Zenith short-wave portable radio, etc.; obtained Venezuelan travel visas; and updated my U.S. passport. My items would be shipped at company expense to my job location in the Lake Maracaibo area. I was also advised that phone calls would not be possible from Venezuela to any foreign countries. Creole Petroleum Corporation, the largest foreign affiliate of Standard Oil Company of New Jersey (which would become EXXON Corp., then Exxon-Mobil Corp.) welcomed me to its Lagunillas, Venezuela, Lake Maracaibo field location in mid-September 1957.

Within two months after returning to my parents' home in San Francisco, my efforts had borne fruit. The same day that I accepted the offer from Standard Oil New Jersey for the amazing job with its major affiliate in Venezuela, I phoned Sandra and we celebrated the news. There remained several weeks of preparation to arrange my departure for Venezuela, but our phone conversations had become about the "when and where" and not "if" regarding the wedding.

The pace of communications between Sandra and me picked up dramatically from occasional phone calls from San Francisco to Gidea Park, U.K., to weekly letters between us from Lagunillas to Gidea Park. My parents were very excited about our wedding plans. I had filled them in with the details of my visit to Sandra's parents and relatives while I was still stationed in Bordeaux. I shared photographs of Sandra with them and all the relatives, which gave rise to countless complimentary remarks and questions about our plans.

I thought that one of the things that had to be done was to purchase an engagement ring and get it to Sandra somehow before I left for Venezuela. Mom helped me shop for and purchase the ring. That was the easy part. We could not find a secure way to get the ring to Sandra. At that time in 1957 there were not the secure means available to mail or ship that exist today. I even foolishly contacted a girl I had been acquainted with eight years prior in high school whom I had heard was planning a trip to England to ask if she might convey the engagement ring to Sandra. That did not turn out to be a great idea.

My father was still permanently employed by the U.S. Naval Office of Civilian Inspectors of Naval Materials and mom continued her job at The City of Paris Department Store, designing and constructing custom-made women's hats. The concept and plan for our wedding in England suggested another long-range planning opportunity for any of the small San Francisco contingent to be included in future traveling plans, which would provide opportunities for visits to Italy.

The American Legacy of an Italian Motorcyclist

20. Welcome to Venezuela

I reported to the field manager on the eastern coast of Lake Maracaibo after landing at the Maracaibo Airport in September 1957. Lagunillas is a small town reachable by a ferry at that time; you would have to cross the narrow neck of "the lake" and then drive an hour-and-a-half south. I was lodged in the bachelors building and shared a room with another young PE who had arrived several months before me. Like many other things in Venezuela, Lake Maracaibo is not what its name suggests. It is a large saltwater bay indirectly connected to the Caribbean Sea. Oil tanker traffic regularly has access to the eastern shore crude oil loading facilities, navigating a network of dredged channels maintained in the rather shallow "lake," whose depth ranges from beaches to 160 feet. It is approximately 100 miles long by 60 miles wide, and leads indirectly to the Caribbean Sea, 10 degrees north of the equator.

213

The American Legacy of an Italian Motorcyclist

During the meeting between myself and the American expatriate Creole Corp. manager, I shared a summary of my PE education and details about my military assignment and personal plans with him. This gentleman was quite frank in counseling me regarding my acclimation to the stressful climate and tolerating the working conditions out on "the lake," where over 4000 oil wells were located, with numerous large "flow-stations" and larger platforms of gas collection, recompression, and injection facilities. All shoreside facilities, from communities, shopping centers, roads, public and private properties and commercial facilities were below sea/lake level by 15 to 20 feet at that time. The lake waters were retained by a miles-long dike constructed and continuously maintained/elevated by companies operating from those eastern shores.

The phenomenon of "subsidence" of the earth's surface adjacent to oilfields is the unavoidable consequence of the withdrawal of gas-saturated crude oil from its deep accumulations over the productive lifetime of almost every oilfield in the world. The combination of the 10 degrees north of the equator and living 15 feet below sea level resulted in extreme working conditions and widespread reliance on air conditioning in most offices and all living quarters. At the conclusion of my welcome-to-Creole conversation with the field manager, he gave me a significant tip: "If you decide at the end of three months that you can tolerate the living and working conditions here, you and other recently arrived employees will be sent to Caracas for a one-month intensive Spanish language class. You may elect to continue Spanish language classes back here on your own time but taught by paid staff instructors. Your quickest way out of here will be to become fluent in Spanish and teach every young Venezuelan to do your job. A newly hired Venezuelan engineer will accompany you on every assignment you will be given. Do a great job and good luck; welcome to Creole Lagunillas!"

Wow, that was some welcome. And the fact was that a very high annual turnover of expatriate employees was a real challenge to management. The expatriate staff far outnumbered the Venezuelan staff; the expatriate staff was well compensated for enduring the living and working conditions but was always figuring how to "get to Caracas" and beyond, ASAP.

I had started studying Spanish in San Francisco the day after I accepted the Venezuelan job. I found it the easiest language to learn that I had ever studied. I stuck it out in Lagunillas for the three months, returned from the crash Spanish course in Caracas, and volunteered to continue Spanish classes for the next year on my own time. I eventually passed the Spanish final written and verbal test one afternoon after work. The instructor left to grade our tests and returned in an hour with a shocked facial expression and announced in a quavering voice: "Se han matado al Presidente Kennedy!" (President Kennedy has been killed!) The date was November 22, 1963.

For the remainder of 1957, my first year on the job, I was rotated through various sections of the field operations while keeping touch with Sandra in London and my parents in San Francisco. I would need to work for 12 months to qualify for my first vacation, leading Sandra to select the date for the wedding to be one week after her 20th birthday. I would arrive with my parents and my mother's sister Erma from San Francisco, the four of us having convened in NYC.

On the day of our arrival in London, Sandra, her sister Sheila and their parents, Cath and Jack, waited at the Liverpool Street Station for me and my relatives. Liverpool Street Station is a huge facility with thousands of air, rail, and road travelers dashing about to meet people or making connections with their next mode of travel or searching for friends or relatives. I left my three family members in search of Sandra as she did likewise looking for me.

After 14 months of separation between Sandra and me, I was searching for an 18-year-old beautiful teenager, and she was searching for a lean lieutenant in uniform. After many minutes of wandering through the mobs of people and having seen dozens of beautiful, long-legged British girls, I almost passed up a particularly stunning young beauty. I paused and turned to see Sandra laughing at me. I had put on a bit of weight having Venezuelan food delivered to the rigs where I was working, and Sandra had become a strikingly gorgeous 20-year-old woman. After hurried introductions of our two families, we all proceeded to Gidea Park, about an hour-and-a-half's drive east of London. Birthday gifts were presented to Sandra while more family members convened, including my favorite Aunt Maria from Turin and my two girl cousins from Milan and Rome, Silvia and Louisanna. Silvia was one of my two Italian girl cousins who had attended our wedding with my Aunt Maria from Turin. Silvia was also the girl who solved Sandra's foot size question a couple of years before when I was on my way to meet Sandra's family in England. All the family visitors from San Francisco and Italy were somehow accommodated in nearby Weevers' neighbors' homes.

It had been resolved that my mom would hang onto the diamond engagement and wedding rings and bring them with her to England in the week before the wedding. That worked out very well, since Mom handed me the ring for Sandra as we arrived in London on Sandra's 20th birthday, making us formally engaged for one week prior to our wedding the following Saturday, September 23, 1958. My wedding gifts to Sandra were a pair of Colombian aquamarines and another of emeralds that I had purchased in Venezuela.

20. Welcome to Venezuela

Our wedding took place in the St. Peter's Episcopal Church of England in South Weald, Essex. During the exchange of vows, a young lad in the altar service heard my voice and exclaimed, "'ee's a Yank!" The Yanks and Italians were a minority at the following wedding reception, given the vast British Weevers' network of aunts, uncles, grandparents, cousins, and friends present the afternoon of the wedding ceremony. My parents and I had planned quite a post-wedding tour of Italy following our two-week honeymoon in Paris and Majorca.

The four of us met in Torino and made a road tour for several days to my father's parents in Boves and my mother's family near Bologna and a few days in Milan, including a jewelry shop in the Milan Galleria del Duomo where Sandra had my gifts of emeralds and aquamarines made into two pairs of earrings. During a break at a cafe we sat down with my parents to review a list of furniture and home supplies we would need to completely furnish one of the scores of homes in the company's family housing development near the offices. The furniture and other items would be purchased in the U.S. by mom and dad and shipped to us as soon as we were assigned the home.

Ranch-style homes of different sizes were available at modest rental fees to staff and professional employees of Creole Corp. The homes were

219

unfurnished with the exception of kitchen appliances. I gave a check to my parents at the cafe meeting to cover the purchases. My parents kindly and happily spent several weeks shopping. With the shopping completed they notified Creole Corp. to collect the entire lot and ship it to us at company expense. Sandra and I spent a few weeks at vacationing friends' homes in Lagunillas awaiting the shipment's arrival. The community of expatriate employees, mostly from the U.S., that I had been befriended by during my solo year were well aware of our plans.

Returning from our honeymoon, the community could not do enough to welcome us into the family circles and rolled out the welcome carpet. When our household shipment arrived, dozens of them turned out to help unload, unpack, and furnish our new home. It was even better than a military environment because they all volunteered to join Creole Corp., continue to work and live there, to have and raise their children there. They provided advice to both of us, particularly from the "ladies to the lady" on how to cope and what to avoid. Mom and dad were eager to get news of the shipment's arrival and learn how everything fit into our first home. The extent and scope of the shipment was astonishing; my parents went well beyond the list of furniture to include kitchen equipment, dining utensils, cutlery, bed linens, blankets, bathroom items, and wedding gifts from San Francisco family and friends in the shipment. Sandra and I merely had to buy groceries at the local supermarket to be self-sufficient.

The company had local Venezuelan doctors and nurses at its large camps of expatriate and local employees along the eastern shore of Lake Maracaibo. The major hospital in the area however, Coromoto, was in the city of Maracaibo on the western shore. A bridge was eventually constructed to connect the two shores of the lake, though it was built years after we moved to Caracas. Prior to the bridge's construction, vehicular traffic from anywhere along the eastern shore to Maracaibo had to endure a haphazard mob of vehicles in numerous lanes crowding and maneuvering against one another to board a limited-capacity ferry. Needless to say, Creole required any expectant mother to be quartered at one of a number of "casitas"—bungalows on Coromoto's campus reserved for pairs of ladies three weeks prior to their anticipated delivery dates.

I soon took Sandra to one of the Coromoto "casitas," already occupied by another Creole employee's wife, to await the birth of Catherine Ann Paredi on June 15th, 1959. I was able to visit Coromoto two or three times during the waiting period and also immediately prior to Catherine's birth. We three returned home to "Tamare," the Creole settlement for its expat employees. Our annual vacation practice for all the remaining years in Venezuela would be to alternate our one-month vacation every year between California and England. We decided to start that practice by visiting San Francisco with "Cat," our first born, in December of 1959 in San Francisco. Mom and dad were thrilled to be grandparents and "oohed" and "aahed" over Cat, who took her first steps at six months of age in the first home that my parents had purchased. It was directly across the street from the home where I had grown up in from 1942 until 1955. Spending Christmas with my family and my grandparents in San Francisco was very special for everyone, especially with our first-born child.

21. Lessons from the Oil Patch

By the time I arrived at Creole's Lake Maracaibo region, its fields off the eastern shore of the lake consisted of approximately 4000 producing wells. Most of these producing fields were over 30 years old. Creole was the largest operator in Venezuela among several other international petroleum corporations. At the time it had the capacity to outproduce Saudi Arabian crude production. My assignments in Creole's aquatic-based operations ranged from being the staff engineer on "workover rigs" to installing water-flood injection platforms and equipment, installing and field testing experimental rotating "screw" pumps, measuring wells' crude and gas volumes, and tracking sources of accidental crude oil leakages polluting the lake's surfaces, shorefronts, and lake bottoms. Creole Corporation pioneered the development of drilling wells from concrete platforms erected in water depths from 30 feet to almost 200 feet. All of its concessions were located over so-called "reservoirs" of different grades of crude oil thousands of feet beneath the lake bottoms, from close to shore to many miles offshore.

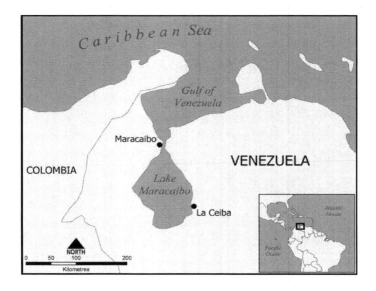

The electro/mechanical infrastructure to support crude oil production from the completed wells spreads out over hundreds of square miles of lake. Thousands of concrete pilings were fabricated, as well as maritime equipment, pile drivers, pipe-laying barges laying thousands of miles of different diameter pipelines, exploration and production-well drilling barges. There were fleets of crew launches operating every eight hours, delivering and retrieving crews working eight-hour shifts day and night, 365 days a year. Thousands of employees were required to staff shipyards, pile casting yards, vast machine shops and materials warehouses. Dozens of basketball court-sized production platforms were erected in the lake to collect the crude flowing or pumped from the 30 or 40 surrounding wells. Four gas collection and recompression plants, each the size of a football field, were erected at strategic locations in the lake to collect and recompress gas separated from crude. This avoided the wasteful practice of "flaring" the unmarketable gas, prolonged the productive lives of the various reservoirs, and increased ultimate total crude recovery of all reservoirs.

Training of petroleum engineers includes assignments on different kinds of wells. Naturally flowing wells don't require pumps to lift crude oil to the surface. Their entrained dissolved gas has the ability to drive the crude oil to the surface without the need of pumps installed at the surface or at the bottom of the wellbore opposite the formation face. As most wells age, they eventually require a down-hole pump at that location, connected to reciprocating machinery at the surface. The ongoing maintenance of any type of well is performed by a "workover rig" equipped with specialized equipment and machinery somewhat different than a "drilling rig." The latter can be stationed on a location for months to a year or more.

AMBROSIO CABIMAS MARACAIBO

In my second year on the lake, I was assigned to a workover rig with the third shift, composed of a crew chief and five Venezuelan roughnecks, the drill crew. We showed up at the workover rig barge by crew launch to relieve the off-going crew at midnight. These men had just finished installing a new bottom-hole pump around 3000 feet of depth at the formation face. It had been many years since the old well flowed naturally, periodically requiring pump maintenance or replacement. The off-going crew had to pause withdrawing the string of 3-1/2" diameter pipe that was open-ended, having replaced the pump. There were 180 feet of pipe still suspended in the hole composed of six 30-foot lengths, all the rest having been withdrawn and stacked within the derrick in 90-foot "stands" of pipe with the help of the derrickman. He was relieved by our derrickman, who soon climbed up to his work platform 90 feet above the derrick floor. The rest of the crew, including the crew boss, called the driller, operated the machinery installed on the platform called the "draw-works," which raised and lowered the pipe-string or rotated it in the hole. My job was to ensure that the crew followed the detailed plan provided by the head PE for every step of the operation and conducted other standard safety procedures before and during the workover procedure. The company's most important standard safety procedure at every shift change in drilling and workover activities is that the oncoming driller test a device called the blowout preventer (BOP), and I observed that he had done so.

All workover and drilling operations produce extremely loud and intermittent noise issuing from a variety of heavy equipment. As the work by my crew continued, withdrawing the remaining tubing string from the well, all hell broke loose and the normal operating sounds of the rig were drowned out by an explosion of incredible, continuous, and painful amplitude. Simultaneously, the 180 feet of pipe-string flew vertically out of the hole, winding itself like cooked spaghetti in and out of the derrick's girders to a height of 100 feet above the "crown" of the derrick. It curled over at the apex of its flight and returned back down, winding itself again through the derrick structure. The last 30 feet of the pipe-string came to rest in a horizontal position 180 degrees opposite the exhaust manifold and muffler of the still-running draw-works. Spewing out over the lake was a steady stream of flammable gas and crude oil, which landed in the lake 50 yards beyond the well platform. This is called a blowout. All of this happened in the same amount of time that it takes to slowly read this sentence.

The noise continued unabated. The derrickman flew from his station 105 feet above the lake as the emerging pipe blasted by his vacated platform. The driller and three roughnecks only had a 15-foot jump into the lake to join the derrickman, who had climbed aboard the rear of the barge. They all remained there, wringing their clothes out. Understandably, not one of the floor crew, including the driller, thought to flip the switch on the platform floor to actuate the BOP. The noise and gushing fluid continued out over the lake.

When the blowout started, I was monitoring the drilling fluid return to its holding and treatment tanks on the barge amidst all the huge pumps circulating the fluid into the wellbore and retrieving it for treatment. The "dog house" is the office of the rig situated at the front right-hand corner of the barge adjacent to the drilling platform. This dog house has a chair, desk, calculator, and the radio, which is the only means of communicating to the operator on her station ashore. The roaring noise continued. I ran across the deck of the barge and up the six steps into the doghouse. I grabbed the handset, signaled the operator, and shouted at her, unable to hear my own voice in Spanish, "Please connect me urgently to Senior Green." Willy Green, the rig's "tool-pusher," my boss of the moment, at about 2 o'clock in the morning, sleepily picked up the phone to hear me shout, "Willie, I've got a blowout underway on well LL-234, please send help!" Willie hung up on me, assuming the call was a practical joke: Workover rigs *never* have blowouts. The noise continued. I called him back immediately and screamed, "Goddammit, Willie, this is no joke! Get your ass out here pronto—we don't know what to do!"

Willie finally showed up about 1-1/2 hours later on a slow launch, laughing. I had no explaining to do because the deafening noise and gushing fluid had eventually stopped, probably before he boarded the launch. More significantly, even though the sky was still dark, the lights on the rig illuminated the evidence wrapped throughout the derrick. Blowouts on workover rigs were never known to happen; this was the first in the history of the 40-

year-old operation. On rare occasions, exploration wells blew out, resulting in fatalities. Willie's terse entry published in the following daily report documenting the status of every rig working on the lake was "Welders cutting drill-pipe from derrick." Nonetheless, we were the butt of well-intended ridicule from all of our friends for several days. We could all have been killed had the gushing, inflammable fluid been ignited by the draw-works exhaust. Normal work on the well continued the following day.

So, what caused the brief but potentially fatal blowout? Might the BOP have stopped the blowout had the driller activated it before going for a short swim? There never was a formal investigation of the ultimately comical and brief incident to determine its cause. The consensus was *subsidence,* which normally accompanies the aging of all oilfields, and causes the surrounding and surface terrain to slowly and continually drop. Once an oilfield is developed, subsidence is absolutely impossible to avoid, reverse, or remedy. As an example, the majority of the eastern coastline of Lake Maracaibo, the edge of the low country, required the building of a miles-long dike and regular increases in its height from year to year. This was essential to prevent extensive flooding of the low country eastward beyond its original lakeshore boundary. Damage to the old well's "surface casings" and surrounding cement probably provided a path over the years for deeper collections of entrapped gas to find their way upward into the atmosphere. The activity of our workover rig over a two-week period certainly disrupted and damaged the integrity of the surface casing system leading to the blowout.

During my vacations to California with my growing family, dad always expressed interest in my work experiences. I never mentioned anything about my workover rig's blowout because it bore no resemblance whatsoever to my father's years of daily confrontations with sudden life-threatening episodes beyond his control during WWI.

What was curious to me were the similarities and differences between dad's and my consideration of exposure at the time to mortal consequences of our assignments. My father knew that he could be severely injured or killed while running his motorcycle to or from the trenches any day or night. The hazard went with the job. Had it happened, he would have been shocked, but not surprised, having had to anticipate the likelihood of it happening day and night for four years.

I, on the other hand, was surprised—shocked, really—to witness my workover rig undergoing a blowout. Blowouts were not known to happen on workover rigs. But when Willie showed up the show was over; it was no joke since there was the evidence: all that 3.5" diameter pipe wound throughout the derrick. Another, but more significant difference between dad's experience and mine was that dad, more than likely, carried the psychological scars of his protracted four-year interlude for some time. He would never bring the subject up of having witnessed blood, carnage, and death at first hand, or having been fearful. In contrast, I can bring up, describe in detail, and laugh about my brief encounter with death that had a lucky outcome.

Another equally significant learning experience that I had while working on the lake had to do with aquatic crude-oil pollution. There was not one recreational beach along the sixty-mile extent of the central eastern shore of Lake Maracaibo. Many of my pals loved fishing. In our occasional spare time we would climb up on the dikes and cast our spinning lures out in the lake. Occasionally, we would catch a fish—and release it, pausing to spray "gas-oil," a solvent, all over our reels' monofilament fishing line, which had become black and sticky, requiring cleaning. A faint crude-oil slick could be seen on the lake's surface for 100 yards facing west up and down the dike front. This was a permanent condition, day in, day out, any time of year.

In our five years of living in Caracas we heard from friends in and out of the oil industry of the fabulous freshwater fisheries in the vast Orinoco River watershed of south-eastern Venezuela.

232

21. Lessons from the Oil Patch

Modern roads were few and terminated at driving distances about 1-1/2 days from Caracas. From that distance to some of the main tributaries of the Orinoco River were nothing but open grassland plains traversed by hundreds of kilometers of dirt roads winding from one isolated village to another, harboring native Venezuelans descended from Indian ancestors raising horses, beef cattle, goats, other livestock, and a myriad of local fruits, corn and vegetables. With the exception of gasoline, these settlements were and are totally self-sufficient.

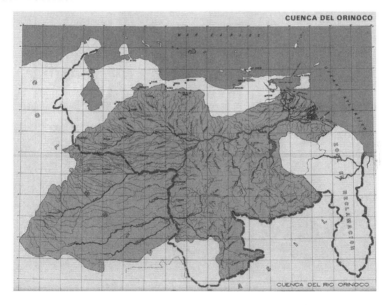

Orinoco River Watershed

The American Legacy of an Italian Motorcyclist

I acquired a surplus Creole geological department's 17-foot aluminum canoe. A close PE pal in the Caracas HQ office and a few other fishing aficionados planned and carried out road trips involving one pal's large, 4-wheel-drive Toyota SUV with my canoe roof-mounted on his vehicle. The challenge of planning and carrying out any kind of fishing trip into that Orinoco tributary "llanos" territory was that the trip could only be undertaken in the very limited dry season, from late December to late February. Any other time of year the thousands of square miles of grassland plains are flooded by torrential downpours that make vehicular and airplane terrestrial access impossible. The only good news for office-working aspiring fishers and hunters considering getting to these areas in the "dry season" was the plethora of religious holidays of three- and four-day weekends afforded by the carefully planned "saints days," which always fell on Mondays and/or Fridays. The guaranteed weeklong "Semana Santa" (Holy Week, before Easter Sunday) also afforded another opportunity for such sportsmen in the dry season.

After a few years of learning the ropes of planning and conducting road-fishing trips into some of these areas, we wondered what opportunity would there be to seek out a means of *flying* into the area in a 4-seater airplane directly from the municipal Caracas airport? My pals agreed to this idea, which would cut off a total of three days' road travel and

21. Lessons from the Oil Patch

make a four-day absence from home into a 3-1/2 days of pure fishing versus three days of road travel for one full day of fishing. We were excited to pursue the idea, and I soon found an aerial survey company owned by a Polish émigré who I invited to visit me at home one weekend. Sr. Boris Kaminsky, a former Olympic kayaking champion and owner of an aerial mapping company, knew everything there was to know about the Orinoco watershed terrain and watercourses, but knew nothing about fishing and was excited about the opportunity to learn to fish it and fly us back to Caracas. He would charge us only for the engine-hours that his four-passenger Cessna 180 registered in getting us there and back, including "hops" from one fishing point to another in a four-day total excursion from Caracas. We would teach him how to fish and furnish all the food and drink and *he would never leave our side* "to come back in four days to pick us up," which we would never have considered. We agreed to plan such trips and flew with Boris to various parts of the watershed for three years of one or two excursions per year in the "dry" season.

There was, however, a somewhat hair-raising part of each of the excursions. The first morning of each four-day excursion we would all show up at the modern Caracas Municipal Airport with our limited amount of camping and fishing gear, load up the Cessna, take off from the paved runways, and fly south for about two hours to a well-equipped small

235

airport to fuel up and continue on to a likely looking small- to medium-sized tributary of a huge tributary to the main Orinoco River, none of the latter we had any desire to fish. We fishermen knew what kind of water and the small tributaries' physical forms would need to be to meet our fishing requirements. Boris had no clue of what such requirements were.

Since the very flatlands of the basin led to very winding paths of all such tributaries, Boris would fly in the zig-zag path up the midline of each until we would select a likely fishing site and Boris would say, "Yes, but look how far you are going to have to hike from that area way up there where I might be able to land, which is going to be a quarter mile or so you would need to hike to get to that spot on the water." In other words, we had to balance our fishing spot needs with Boris' requirements for a likely safe landing spot. We soon learned how to give priority to a safe landing area. It did not take long to let Boris select a probable safe landing area reasonably near a likely fishing area. We would soon find a spot that was acceptable and Boris would say, "Okay, we are gonna drag the strip I would like to land on at a moderate speed but not land. If there are no obstacles in that tall grass, we will loop around and shoot a landing. The strip we land on will be the same we will take off from and needs to have no trees at either end which would impede a safe take-off."

Well, we never really understood what we were getting into when discussing these feasibilities in Caracas. But now we were here and we, including Boris, had a choice. This was a real test of confidence between three of us ignoramuses of flying and landing and the knowledge of a professional flier and lander. We took off and landed on such terrain several times in three days and only once in three years did we hear the stall-warning buzzer going off as we approached a wall of trees at the end of a takeoff "runway." One other time we had a heavy weight of fresh fish we wanted to try and return home with and Boris gave us an alternative. He could take one of us and the fish to an intermediate "good looking strip," unload the one of us with the fish, return to the original strip, pick up the two remaining, go back to the temporary strip, reload all, and return to Caracas. Okay, good deal, let's do that! Looking back on that I think we were pushing our luck! Maybe that was an example of "mass machismo?"

Two hours' fishing in an Orinoco tributary, with a great catch
of Peacock bass ("Eye-spot" cichlids) and payara

21. Lessons from the Oil Patch

Two things happened that really shook me up while we lived in Venezuela.

One of my PE friends, senior to me, got off the crew launch after a shift and was shot and killed on the dock by one of his Venezuelan laborers. My friend was an Irish gentleman with a wife and three kids. I happened to need an automobile and purchased it from his widow. We were not close friends but in that environment everyone knew one another.

A worse incident involved a closer friend and recent PE arrival from Oklahoma, Terry Morrison. Terry had never seen an ocean before and became so fascinated with "big water" that he joined the Lake Maracaibo Yacht Club, learned how to sail, and bought a second-hand "STAR" two-person, fixed-keel Olympic-class sailboat with "running back-stays," which I knew nothing about. Terry had married a beautiful Tex/Mex young lady, Rosalie, who taught in one of our bilingual company primary schools.

On a Saturday morning, Terry knocked on our door in the same "bedroom camp" where we lived and invited me to accompany him and expectant Rosalie to go sailing together on his recently refurbished "Star" sailboat off the Maracaibo Yacht Club marina in town. My wife, Sandra, and our girls had left for our annual one-month holiday to her parents in England two weeks before I was to follow them. I was thrilled to be invited and jumped at the chance. Terry was the skipper and Rosalie knew how to carefully handle the "running back-stays" that kept the mainmast from breaking in half before the skipper warned he was about to change directions. Almost monthly such an accident was reported in the local papers.

Rosalie handled the mainstays and passed several beers back and forth throughout the sail. I just sat low in the bilge and watched what the two of them did while we drank beers and had a good time. We were heading downwind on a "broad-reach" with the mainsail "boom" at a right-angle to the mainmast, as the wind speed increased at a very fast pace.

Terry invited me to "take over the helm" and change places with him so I could feel what it was like to "sail so fast on a beautiful afternoon." I demurred and had not noticed that he asked Rosalie to reach back and hold the tiller steady, holding the boat on course. He then decided to walk toward me on the portside gunnel to trade places with me, while he expected me to head back to take command of the tiller from Rosalie. Terry was slowly approaching me to exchange places and, with no warning, lost his balance and fell into the lake. There were no flotation devices on board and we didn't think to throw the beer-cooler overboard.

21. Lessons from the Oil Patch

I had no choice but to hop back and relieve Rosalie of the tiller and hold the boat on course while she continued to manage the backstays. Before we knew it we were proceeding at speed downwind and were several hundred yards beyond Terry, who had to stay afloat somehow out in the middle of the lake. We had to quickly turn about and tack, zig-jagging upwind towards Terry, with Rosalie repeatedly switching the running backstays to avoid breaking the mainmast, placing all of us in danger, and losing sight of Terry, and of course we had no communications aboard.

As we finally approached Terry we shot straight past him, leaving him in our wake because I had no idea how to stop the boat to pick him up. We had to repeat the whole procedure once more by reversing course upwind of Terry, sailing past him again downwind, unable to stop and reversing course again. I finally figured out how to stop the boat nearing Terry while going up-wind by simply pointing the boat into the wind and letting go of the tiller. We hauled an exhausted Terry into the boat. He had grabbed several coconuts floating on the lake to help him stay afloat. That was the fun part of our relationship. We mentioned little or nothing of the near catastrophe to our friends at the office or camp.

Terry had tired of the PE work for Creole, and on one vacation back to Oklahoma with Rosalie decided to learn how to make pork sausages in the

241

Maracaibo area on their return. He located the sources of pigs and bought an old surplus Creole ambulance to transport them to be slaughtered and butchered not far from our residential camp. He produced the sausages at home to market them to Maracaibo's numerous restaurants, all the while tending to his PE assignments on the lake. Apparently, the existing Venezuelan native sausage makers in town decided they did not need his competition and Terry was murdered. It just so happened that his parents had been visiting them —Rosalie and their two children. Terry's venture came to a quick and tragic end and his family immediately returned to Oklahoma. A very small report of Terry's murder appeared in the local paper. There never was any further news regarding Terry's murder or its investigation by the Venezuelan authorities, as there was never any such news in the murder of our Irish coworker.

22. My Parents' Dream Move

Several years after returning to his position with the U.S. Navy as an Inspector of Naval Materials in San Francisco, dad was offered a transfer to Monterey, California. The U.S. armed services had for many years established foreign languages schools there for various branches of the service's members. Proficiency in a particular foreign language would be required of them prior to their permanent assignment abroad. By the mid-1950s almost all branches of the services had a growing need of such training for particular members being posted to foreign locations. The U.S. Navy was embarking on a significant expansion of its foreign language training facility in Monterey. Dad's assignment there was to inspect all construction materials to be employed in expanding the living and instruction quarters of the facility. My parents were familiar with the beautiful Monterey Peninsula and had good friends who had been

243

living there for several years. It was a wonderful opportunity and an easy decision to make. They sold their home in San Francisco and purchased a lovely three-bedroom home in Seaside, a neighboring town to Monterey.

Mom and dad in the 1950s

22. My Parents' Dream Move

In the meantime, Sandra, Cat, and I had returned to Lagunillas, Venezuela, for me to go back to work with Creole Petroleum Corp. Our next year's holiday took place in Gidea Park, U.K., at Christmastime, to introduce Cat and Jacqueline, our second daughter, to their grandparents, Jack and Cath Weevers, and their extended family. During the years between 1958 and 1964 our young family rotated our annual vacations between Monterey and Gidea Park. The grandparents at each location got to see their grandchildren every two years. Sandra and I took advantage of the grandparents' babysitting "privileges" to take ski trips to France, Austria, and Switzerland.

Mom and dad took great pride in their new home in the Monterey area and, over the years living there, invested hours of labor transforming the home and garden to their liking. Always knowing ahead of time of our planned summertime vacation visits, dad spent much of his spare time preparing the garden area of the home's back yard to build a swing set and other attractions for their grand-daughters. He was particularly proud of the four-foot high scale model of a mountain he built from his recollections of his boyhood in Piedmonte, Italy. The model was built into a corner of the wooden fence around the lower backyard lawn and had water running down from its summit of "melting snow" to a little lake, the water being pumped back up to circulate continually when switched on.

The American Legacy of an Italian Motorcyclist

Dad's "mountain" being enjoyed by my daughters and a friend

On another holiday my parents took the girls, at four and five years old, to a local rodeo in Salinas, a nearby town in the valley.

Sandra and I spent several of those summertime visits traveling to northern California with a fraternity brother of mine. Glenn Delisle, his wife, and four similarly aged daughters would join us with our girls at mountain resorts in the high Sierras on camping and fishing trips. On one of the trips my parents followed the gang and enjoyed motel rooms and room service as the two families

22. My Parents' Dream Move

with six young girls enjoyed the camping experience: a campfire, midnight star-gazing, and an Indian reservation's swimming pool/resort. Glenn and I took off one day to trout fish at a distant river, leaving the two mothers and six girls at the Indian resort.

Dad's job in Monterey included the inspection of all construction materials for the Navy Foreign Language School expansion. Testing of concrete was an important task to assure its compressive strength prior to a batch being poured for a foundation or wall. The test samples were cylinders four inches in diameter and one foot in length. Dad would witness the compression test and would reject a batch of concrete if it did not meet the required specifications. Over the course of a few years dad collected hundreds of the cylinders that had passed the test. He would load them in the trunk of his car and take them home instead of sending them to the town dump.

He used those perfectly sound concrete cylinders to construct four-foot high retaining walls down the steep slope of the back yard to create five-foot wide garden terraces, which were then planted with flowering shrubs or vegetables. Two flights of stairs separated the three sets of terraces on each side descending to the lawn, where the girls' swing set and mountain model were located. Every several years, sections of the six concrete cylinder retaining walls needed adjusting due to water seepage down the slope of the back yard. He did it all. Dad's approach was to do it himself if he knew how to do it or learn how if he didn't.

Views of dad's garden

22. My Parents' Dream Move

My father was a good draftsman and decent artist. He decided to paint large surfaces facing the backyard, such as the garage doors and stucco rear walls of the home. His subjects ranged from simulated flower boxes to large scenes of his childhood village's central square, with its monuments, buildings, and plantings. He and mom would host occasional barbecue parties for friends and neighbors on the upper level of the garage garden surrounded by the paintings, of which he was very proud.

In front of Nino's mural, from left to right: Jacqueline, Cat, my mother, my father, and Sandra, 1975

249

The American Legacy of an Italian Motorcyclist

23. My Dream Transfer

In the summer of 1964, I was transferred to the Creole Petroleum Engineering Department Headquarters in Caracas, Venezuela. We rushed to find a home to ensure that our daughters would be able to start school at the beginning of the fall semester. We were now "on the economy" and Creole was no longer required to find housing for the HQ staff.

After a few weeks I saw a prospective home for rent within walking distance of the 10-story Creole HQ building in one of the best downtown neighborhoods of Caracas. A quick meeting with the home's Italian immigrant owner to check the property was arranged. Our family met Sr. Monzeglio at Caracas' most spectacular looking residence at that time, Quinta Olari. Quinta Olari was built on the edge of a ridge facing due north overlooking the valley of Caracas, with its

251

The American Legacy of an Italian Motorcyclist

numerous family neighborhoods and commercial buildings.

Two views of Quinta Olari

23. My Dream Transfer

The home was a four-story structure suspended over the city street below by two massive pre-stressed concrete arms at a 45-degree angle connected to the halfway point of the main floor of the home two stories above the garden, with three more stories rising from the main floor to the roof of the building. It was one of the first buildings in Latin-America to employ pre-stressed concrete in its structure.

Our main concern was the internal architecture of the ultra-modern home of 14-foot ceilings. There were two flights of "floating stairs" between each floor that were not connected to the walls. Banisters at the outside edges of the eight flights of stairs were of no concern. However, the inside edges of all the stairs were not attached to the walls, leaving a four-inch space from the very top of the flights down to the garden level of the lowest flight. Visualize dropping a tennis ball from the space between the topmost step and the wall and watching the ball drop freely until bouncing at the garden level floor. Our daughters thought it funny. I, with my limited fluency in Italian, chatted with Sr. Monzeglio to express our anxiety regarding the weird and possibly unsafe stairs. The fact was that Sandra loved the place and Sr. Monzeglio was desperate to rent it to anyone but a Venezuelan. A relatively low rental was agreed to; we lived in the home for five years and hosted some of the most wonderful parties for our expat friends and workmates in Caracas. Several terraces of gardens below the home led to a tennis-court-sized illuminated bocce-ball court that provided plenty of merriment for after-dinner parties. The home was internationally known in architectural circles and was featured in a *National Geographic* magazine article in 1964. On occasion, tourists would ring the doorbell seeking admission to what they thought was some kind of museum. I eventually discovered that one of my college-mates at U.C.-Berkeley, an architecture major, had won a graduate stipend to tour Latin America investigating interesting structures and had photographed the home.

Sandra and me, Christmas 1967

23. My Dream Transfer

Appropriate family housing was provided to Venezuelan labor force workers where necessary in adjoining areas to the professional-level employees near each of the several operating fields. The Venezuelan labor force workers were typically non-English speakers and the expat professional employees spoke Spanish with varying degrees of fluency. Every one of the shore-bound "camps" of dwellings had access to Venezuelan villages or small towns, which had the usual social and domestic amenities, including restaurants, movie theaters, supermarkets, small shops, and service company housing for the many specialized companies such as Halliburton, Schlumberger, Cameron, etc.

The young Venezuelan professionals, having graduated from American or Venezuelan universities, tended to socialize among themselves and had the benefit of their parents, relatives, and classmates to afford themselves the sense of being home while developing the Venezuelan economy. I became extremely friendly with young Venezuelan computer programmers in Caracas who contributed immensely to my ability to eventually be promoted in 1969 to Standard Oil Corp.'s HQ Mathematics & Computer Sciences Department in New Jersey.

Several of our American expat bachelor friends married American Creole English/Spanish-speaking schoolteachers from its bilingual schools

255

in the field and Caracas. Some of the young men met and married young ladies in Caracas of Venezuelan families, including some of German descent whose parents fled Germany after WWII.

There was a bonding phenomenon among all professional levels of Creole employees that continued throughout the years of its existence, which covered the years between the early 1930s to the early '80s. All of the expat corporations' petroleum concessions were then voluntarily returned to the Venezuelan government. There had been annual Creole Employee Reunions held in large American cities for years prior to the industry's nationalization that were week-long events, with golf competitions, social events, banquets, and presentations by EXXON executives. The Creole spirit was similar to that of American military veterans, which transcended the rank, age, and geographic origin of its employees. In later years, the reunions seemed to include as many adult children of its employees as EXXON/Creole retirees. The reunions ceased when the Creole retirees were outnumbered by their children!

At the office in Caracas, I found that my colleagues were petroleum reservoir engineers highly skilled in advanced mathematics and computer programming. They were primarily engaged in creating complex mathematical models to run on huge IBM computers in the Creole HQ computer center. I had never seen a computer, let alone programmed one. I spent five years studying engineering, including advanced math, until graduating in 1955; I and all other engineering students carried 10-inch slide rules every day to class to tediously solve complex math problems. Nuclear engineering problems critical to the development of nuclear energy and the atomic bomb had been carried out for years in the top-secret, computer-equipped center atop a ridge of the Berkeley Hills overlooking the U.C. campus. In Caracas I assisted the senior PEs for a year in "validating" the simulated oil production of particular petroleum reservoirs under Lake Maracaibo. We would compare a reservoir's simulated production to historically recorded actual annual production and alter the mathematical values of the reservoirs' properties until running the model would match its actual production over past time periods. The model would then be regarded a valid tool to run into the future with different investment scenarios. I learned the FORTRAN computer programming language and created a few applications that helped other engineers at the HQ office speed up their analytic tasks.

However, I kept thinking about the massive amount of production data from the over 4000 wells in the Lake Maracaibo fields that were accumulating in hand-posted paper files. For seven years I had worked with that data hand-entered in the thick old-fashioned files. Solutions to problems pertaining to specific sets of wells in a specific reservoir were time consuming, inefficient, and error prone. No two wells were the same with regard to age, downhole or surface equipment, the volumes of gas and crude produced, the grade of crude: how difficult were they to bring back into production after having been shut down for days or months? Creole's production operation was a "swing producer," meaning that it responded from day to day to the changing needs for different grades of crude required by its customers or its own refineries. The managers of each separate section of the fields had to make quick decisions every day to respond to the varying volumes of crude required and to determine which wells to open or close.

In the course of my training assignments at other U.S. locations of Standard Oil of New Jersey Corporation, I was fascinated with the telecommunication equipment and applications (computer programs) being used to transfer data from refineries to the large computer centers, where reports were generated and transmitted back to the refineries to improve their operations. I realized the huge opportunity Creole HQ Engineering Department had if it were feasible to create computer applications to be run in the HQ computer center overnight and to return useful reports the following day to field production managers.

Upon my return to Caracas from a two-week training assignment in the U.S., I called my pals back in the Lake Maracaibo oil production offices, made appointments with them and flew out, accompanied by Comptrollers Department computer programmers, for several visits. My team gained the support of the field production engineers and management to develop a pilot project for a small sector of the huge oilfields, composed of several flow stations' platforms and a few hundred of their wells. Caracas Comptrollers Department agreed to provide the support of its COBOL computer language programmers, who maintained the computer programs that produced the existing monthly reports, which had little practical value to field operations managers.

Everyone connected with the pilot project became committed and excited about the promise of new daily reports that they themselves defined during the early stages of the project. Telecommunication engineers in Caracas HQ assured me that the unlimited capacity of the 400-mile long microwave-based tower system between the Lake Maracaibo operation and Caracas could be used to transmit data. Volumes of raw data from the field transmitted to Caracas and unlimited volumes of end-user specified reports returned daily would be feasible. I selected the types of new IBM equipment that would be needed in both locations, their relatively minimal rental costs and delivery times, necessary operators' training needs in the field, and in Caracas. Creole top management support from the field units and Caracas was forthcoming.

The Venezuelan computer programmers proficient with the COBOL computer language and I flew on Creole aircraft as necessary to meetings in the field with production department engineers. The latter were to be the clients of the pilot project and would ultimately determine its use and utility to them in their daily occupations. The clients' requests for specific formats and contents of every one of dozens of daily reports were never deemed impossible or rejected by the computer application's programmers. We always found a way.

From the time that I conceived the idea of the pilot project to the time of its implementation in Caracas and field locations, it took about a year and a half to launch. In less than three months' use of the system by the production department field staff, the client group deemed it a total success. Top management of the department demanded its expansion to cover the entire field of the Lake Maracaibo production operations, disregarding cost. The additional IBM equipment required at both locations—Caracas and field—was approved and ordered. Within three more months, the production operations management in the Lake

260

23. My Dream Transfer

Maracaibo fields never looked back: more applications were conceived by field operations, leading to development of a local computer center and support staff dedicated to the production organization's needs.

I immediately suspected who would head up the first computer center in the field.

Me, Cat, Jacqueline, Sandra

24. Return to America

Sandra and I contemplated our future if we were to remain in Venezuela. Our girls were in the third and fourth grades of the bilingual Creole-Caracas elementary school. It was the practice of the expat Creole employees working in Venezuela who had children to send them off to boarding schools in the U.S. once they reached "middle-school" age. For a variety of reasons that scenario did not appeal to us. Also, the long-term political direction of the country was showing signs of weakening as the 1970s were approaching.

In 1966, a high-level executive, Donald Drier, was transferred from ARAMCO Saudi Arabia to the Creole Comptrollers department in Caracas. Don was among the many American expats who joined the Caracas Tennis Club. Our favorite sport was tennis and the Creole bunch of CTC members of all ages and levels of employment made friends easily, particularly when many of them were decent tennis

263

players, as were Don and his wife. Don's specific goal at the Creole HQ, ironically enough, was to improve the relationship between the Comptrollers Department and the Engineering Department. An underlying issue between the two departments was the need for the Engineering Department to require exclusive use of the whole HQ computer center during its third shift due to the excessive computer processing power required by Engineering's reservoir simulation models. In the meantime, I was developing the successful pilot project supporting the Lake Maracaibo production activity. Don became very acquainted with the progress and success of the pilot project early in the course of his three-year assignment in Caracas. In 1968, Don was transferred to the SONJ Corporation in Florham Park, New Jersey, to help establish a brand new corporate HQ unit called the Mathematics and Computer Systems Department.

It became known in Creole HQ that Mobil Oil Corp. was trying to recruit me for a position in its Italian affiliate's location in Rome. Mobil flew me to NYC over a weekend to be interviewed for the Italian position. I returned with no expectation of getting an offer. The extremely liberal compensation plan all expat employees enjoyed in Venezuela, being paid 14-month's salary for 11 months of work, could not be matched anywhere else in the world, let alone Italy. Several months after returning from the Mobil Corp. visit, I was offered a position in

24. Return to America

Florham Park, in the brand new SONJ HQ Mathematics and Computer Systems Department. Don Drier turned out to be more than a friend. He got me transferred out of Venezuela.

The young Paredi family bid a fond farewell to all our pals in Caracas, packed up, and arrived in New Jersey in the late summer of 1969. I had spent 12 years in Venezuela, 11 years of them married with a British wife and two daughters, Venezuela-born citizens. Once again, we urgently searched for and found a home in New Providence, NJ, a 20-minute drive from Florham Park, in time for our growing girls to start their American schooling, a 10-minute walk from home. My parents made immediate plans to visit New Jersey, as did Sandra's parents in Gidea Park, England. Our vacation schedules to both grandparents' homes were adjusted.

After several weeks of settling in at the new SONJ "Math and Computer Sciences Department," I was directed to head up a study team to determine what had gone wrong with the new department's computer operations center. The new corporate HQ level department was created for many reasons, including to absorb the computer operations functions of two large corporate HQ-level computer centers at other relatively nearby locations, NYC and Florham Park, NJ. The new MCS Department also centralized commercial activities supported by large commercial computer applications in the payroll, accounting, logistical, and computer simulation systems developed by the refinery support organization Esso Research and Engineering Department (ER&E). Computer applications in these disparate areas running on different brands of computers resulted in a challenging mix of computer users running important computer applications on different brands and types of computer hardware—in short, a nightmare. The physical facility housing the new MCS Department was a brand new three-story building accommodating close to 400 staff and a brand new spacious computer center.

I got to know several of the computer center operations staff during the first several weeks after my arrival at the new MCS organization. I was able to hand-pick three members to help me with the study. They were well regarded by their peers and different levels of management in the department. My team quickly developed the terms of reference and scope of its investigation and developed a wide-ranging set of interviews between the team members, computer operations, and users of the computer center's services. The team's study was concluded in less than a month's time, with its recommendations presented privately to the top two managers in the computer operations area. Within a week of the conclusion of the study, I presented our conclusions to top MCS management. I was immediately promoted and

24. Return to America

assigned to lead a reorganized computer operation section by implementing all of the study group's recommendations. Those included physical changes to the computer center layout, restrictions and control of access to the computer center, and guidelines for accepting certain applications being run at certain times of the day or night shifts during the normal 24/7 operation. A series of team-building and organizational development seminars was also launched using outside organizational development consultants to improve personal interactions among and between the various sections of the Computer Operations Division. I established and headed early morning meetings with computer operations leaders and RCA and IBM employees/technicians. Regular, measured steps were taken in the organization such that in one year the prioritized measures were in place, and by the end of the second year I requested a new assignment.

The vacations with grandparents were now limited in duration compared to the months-long visits to England and California when our young family had lived and worked in Venezuela. But one visit of several weeks by Sandra's mother and father was especially memorable.

Cath and Jack, Sandra's parents, embarked on the QE 2 cruise ship in the fall one year from London, destination NYC. We met them and installed them in our guest bedroom in New Providence, New

Jersey. Sandra and I planned an itinerary starting in the Delaware River Valley, about a two-hour drive west, for a day or two. A high point for Jack was his ordering a famous Irish beer in a quaint lodge along the river and finding it to be a genuine Irish Guinness import, not the English variety of Guinness made in Britain for the English market and considered inferior compared to the "real thing." And Jack loved T-bone steak. One of the visits was to our vacation property on Long Beach Island, New Jersey. A locally famous steak-house restaurant was one of our favorite spots. One evening we scheduled dinner there and I suggested that Jack try the special T-bone dinner. The British version of the dish was a modest-sized steak, probably a vestige of the WWII post-war recovery years. Jack was flabbergasted when his dinner arrived with the T-bone hanging over the edges of the sizable oblong dinner plate festooned with veggies and fries. He couldn't stop talking about it for the rest of their visit.

The New England fall is a special time of year in America, with the spectacular forests' rainbow of colors throughout a swath of states in northern New England that hold all visitors in awe of the annual spectacle. About one week of their visit was dedicated to a "fall foliage tour" of New England, which involved many miles of driving long distances from northern New Jersey. After returning from our road trip one evening, a day or

24. Return to America

two prior to Cath and Jack's departure for England, Cath remarked that it had been such a pleasure to have visited such a huge area of America. I mentioned that the area driven was but a minor part of America and brought out the Rand McNally atlas. I turned to the page showing the whole of the U.S. and showed Cath the sector we all had driven through, from New Jersey to eastern Pennsylvania up through a part of New England and back. Cath was astonished to the point of disbelief that they had visited such a tiny area of America.

For one of my parents' visits from Monterey, during the time when the Twin Towers were still dominating the New York City skyline, my mom and dad visited us at our home in New Jersey. I had planned a dinner for us at the Windows on World restaurant atop one of the towers. Upon finishing our meal, I suggested to my parents and Sandra that they allow me a head start of 10 minutes or so to retrieve our car from a nearby parking facility. I paid the bill and proceeded to the elevator. After a brief wait, the elevator arrived with one passenger, and out stepped Jackie Kennedy, the most famous and alluring widow in the world. She looked me straight in the eye; my jaw did not drop but my slight smile of recognition may have been noticed.

The American Legacy of an Italian Motorcyclist

25. Traveling, Headquarters Projects

Corporate HQ staff work introduced a totally different kind of working environment and range of possible assignments. Between 1964 and 1969, I traveled for training and project development purposes from Caracas to New York, New Jersey, Louisiana, and Texas. From 1969 to 1981 I visited locations in western and eastern Canada, London, Brussels, Florida, Wyoming, California, Norway, and Colombia for special projects and foreign EXXON Regions project coordination work. A six-week training course on petroleum reservoir engineering in Houston brought me in contact with a young fellow student who spent a short time in Caracas and then went on to become the CEO of EXXON Corp. EXXON foreign regional senior staff from every part of the world regularly attended computer center management topics I covered in annual meetings in Florham Park, NJ.

The American Legacy of an Italian Motorcyclist

From 1969 to 1985 my assignments ranged from computer operations management to a large variety of staff assignments, including major coordination work for corporate HQ departments, coordination and development of intraregional computer security guidelines, initiation and development of annual meetings of major region's computer operations managers, and stewardship of Esso-Europe's investment in MYCRON, a Norwegian independent research startup company's project to develop the world's first single board microcomputer. The latter project was one of several Norwegian non-petroleum industry ventures that Esso-Europe financed as a part of the bidding process for petroleum exploration concession awards to permit exploration drilling in the Norwegian sector of the North Sea.

Norway was the first nation in the world to institute the imaginative idea of including in the concession awarding process more than "the highest cash bidder." Norway developed a large list of non-petroleum-related enterprises for hopeful concession bidders, providing capital support in addition to cash to win concessions. Four such Norwegian startup ventures were added to Esso-Europe's bids, which made the difference in winning particular concession exploration drilling permits. Three of the activities were assigned to EXXON's U.S. domestic affiliate in Houston and one was assigned to EXXON Corp. HQ to support.

25. Traveling, Headquarters Projects

Consequently I was assigned to "steward" the $20M project for an undetermined period. It started with the task of establishing the legal framework for the Esso European Region and MYCRON project. Esso-Europe's role was to provide the funds over the course of the project, not in one lump payment. After my two-month task of developing the legal framework defining the project and payment method, I established a schedule of meetings between the steering committee of Esso-Europe, my EMCS HQ department, and MYCRON management. The committee would review the progress of the project and approve payments to MYCRON to sustain the project to its completion or exhaustion of the fund. It took four years for the little company to spend the capital that helped it develop its single-board computer. I conducted the quarterly meetings of the committee in either Oslo or Tromso, Norway.

The latter city has an impressive history for such a relatively small coastal town. After the conclusion of WWII, Tromso attained NATO's attention due to the role it played in that war as a result of Germany's invasion and occupation of Norway. The country was easily invaded from its top by the Germans, who, starting from Murmansk, Russia, proceeded down the entire length of 1,090-mile-long Norway in a matter of months. The first significant town the Germans over-ran was Tromso. The country's ocean waters off its coast had remained ice free for centuries, making Tromso the favorite departure and return port of

25. Traveling, Headquarters Projects

Arctic and Antarctic maritime explorers seeking the north and south poles of the planet. This phenomenon also made the town a critical resource, post-WWII, for NATO's investment in a highly sophisticated sea-bottom installation of a cable network designed to capture and record the unique sonic "prints" of every ship that passes to and from the Atlantic Ocean. Thereby, every Russian military or commercial vessel's engine room's prints was captured, recorded, and shared as necessary with NATO members. A large community of NATO marine intelligence operatives was eventually quartered near the new campus of the Norwegian Tromso University.

One summer we scheduled our annual family holiday to England following a quarterly steering committee meeting in Tromso. My primary Norwegian contact at MYCRON was a young Norwegian engineer, Alv Elvestad, recently returned to Norway after graduate work at Dartmouth College in New Hampshire. Leaving our daughters in the care of Sandra's parents in England, Sandra accompanied me to Tromso, which allowed the two of us a few weeks' tour of Norway from north to south. Alv, being a native of the Tromso region, invited the two of us on his brother's motor canoe for a four-day trip up the Reisa River, which forms a border of a national park, through the mountainous inland areas of the region. This area is regularly traversed by native

275

The American Legacy of an Italian Motorcyclist

Lap reindeer "herders" and their families who follow the national migration of thousands of the animals that have been wandering between the northern reaches of Norway, Sweden, and Finland for eons. Every day of our upstream canoe transit we would go around a bend in the river and suddenly come upon a spectacular waterfall hundreds of meters high cascading into the river. We would pull ashore and wander around, have a brief snack, and proceed upstream. Beyond every turn of the river we would take in the view of another spectacular waterfall and verdant surrounding vegetation. Every evening we would find a small secured cabin for which Alv had been lent the key by the forestry manager, so we had bunks and a wood-fired stove to conclude the day's spectacular travel in an unspoiled wonderland of water, wildlife, and forests.

During my fall, winter, and spring meetings in southern and northern Norway, my hosts spent much time cross-country skiing, weather permitting. They always invited me to join them for many memorable experiences. The hills around Oslo include over 2000 kilometers of tended winter ski trails. One excursion was undertaken an hour's drive north of Oslo to take advantage of better snow conditions. All of Norway's tended ski trails or open country slopes were rarely flat but for short stretches, and totally unlike my normal flat trails in NJ along creek-beds or closed-for-the-

25. Traveling, Headquarters Projects

winter golf courses. The three MYCRON couples picked me up at my Oslo hotel for the drive north, where they parked at the foot of a large mountain and unloaded the car trunks and loaded up backpacks for every man and woman, save me.

I noticed the large backpacks had plenty of extra room, which was overloaded with several fire-logs before packing in the food and drink. I was curious about all the extra weight in the backpacks, and was told that every spring most families would take their children of all ages for a one- or two-week skiing excursion into the hills. The family would ski all day from point to point, setting up a camp for the night and searching for enough wood for a fire. So this day trip was purposely overloaded to keep the adults in shape for their real holidays with kids who might not be able to carry much weight in their backpacks.

Okay, so we seven set off uphill for about three hours, stopping once in a while for a drink, chat, or to admire the view. I struggled, but managed to keep up. Finally around noon after the predominately uphill trek we reached a clearing with surrounding trees and settled down on the snow around a canvas spread on the ground for the picnic of wonderful local sandwiches and heated-up lemonade or cold water. After the hour lunch break we gathered up to return downhill to the cars. One of the women was designated to follow me back down, always staying behind and above me. The other women and husbands took off at speed downhill to await us at the cars.

After about an hour downhill skiing, I was getting more comfortable with the totally different technique of downhill skiing with cross-country skis. At the next stop I turned to look up the slope and watched Inga, the manager's wife who was following me, catch an edge on a turn and crash bigtime, with skis flying off in all directions. I was alarmed and turned back to ski uphill to join Inga, who had calmly collected her gear and skis. She had a large sharp hunting knife in hand and was busily shaving the splinters off the broken end of the one ski that had lost its toe. She seemed totally in control and not excited or alarmed, and I greeted her by saying something stupid like, "Wow, are you Okay; may I help you?" She replied, "No, no, I'm fine; how are you? I will be ready to join you in a few moments after I fit this plastic spare ski-toe over the broken end of my ski and then we may continue. Sorry for the delay." An hour later, we rejoined the group at the parked cars and not much was made over our delay or the broken ski. The backpacks were unloaded of their logs and a wonderful outing was enjoyed safely by all.

One night in Oslo after the meeting, a few of the MYCRON men invited me to join them around 10 p.m. to ski part of the downhill trails within the metropolitan boundary of Oslo. These trails are illuminated at night with electric lights. We got to the top of the run, bright lights and all, suited up, and took off downhill, stopping along the way to catch a breath. About 1 a.m., suddenly, no lights! Fortunately for me, there were no clouds and some moonlight, so I very closely followed the man ahead of me, who slowed down a bit, and we made it back to someone's home for akvavit and hot soup and all was well. On a crowded weekend on those same slopes little old Norwegian women would be conducting a group of young children up or down the ski slopes and passing me up at high speeds along the way. Every public or private conveyance winter or summer has ski-holder racks mounted fore and aft. In that summertime when Sandy and I toured Norway, partly by bus in the mountains, we would come across small groups of skiers whose skis were outfitted with wheels fore and aft and whose ski poles had rubber tips to engage the pavement to help push the skier up the paved surfaces of the two-laned mountain roads. On the downhill runs we presumed they would remove the skis and walk down the steep grades.

In the wintertime along the coast, local residents invented the frozen ocean sport of sea-ice skating. This entails wearing heavy insulated boots mounted on heavy duty ice hockey-like skates, heavy insulated clothing and similar extra clothing, and a large dry towel in a backpack. The backpack straps are each fitted at armpit levels with a grommet loop which holds an icepick. The two icepicks are connected with a length of cord loosely looped behind the skater's neck. This is not a solo sport. The idea is to suit up and skate over the surface of the sea ice as far as one can go straight out from the frozen shore, until you are tired or fall through an unfrozen patch of ice. In the latter case, up to your neck in unfrozen sea water, you calmly grab an icepick in each hand from the shoulder straps and reach back to still-frozen ice, drive the icepicks through the first frozen ice you can find, haul your body out on the solid ice, take all your clothes off as quickly as possible, dry your body with the hopefully dry towel, clothe yourself with the dry clothes from the backpack, say a few prayers, and retrace your path back to shore.

Norwegians are a unique race with a restrained sense of humor and a devoted sense of camaraderie. They are party animals. At a dinner party of many couples, a man across the table from you or at the far end of the table from you and your wife or girlfriend, may shout out: "Sandra, skol!" He will be holding a glass of akvavit and your wife or girlfriend is obliged to hold her glass of the liquor up and respond, "Skol!" and toss down the contents. Since akvavit, the Norwegian celebratory liquor, looks like water but kicks like 40-proof vodka, a popular but wise woman will replace her glass's contents with water ASAP!

My Norway assignment turned out to be the most enjoyable of my EXXON career. Sandra and I made

25. Traveling, Headquarters Projects

very good friends there in the company I was helping; one of them, Alv Elvestad, resettled in New Hampshire with his American wife and family. The regular travel to Norway via London gave me chances to see Sandra's family, since the air-route to Oslo required a flight change-over in London. Depending on the quarterly meetings' calendar I was sometimes able to visit London for a weekend. The conventional flight departure schedules from New York occasionally were overloaded, and I was offered the choice of a Concorde aircraft seat— leaving a bit later but getting to London much sooner; this occurred four times and I never complained. (Don't laugh: one of my department's vice presidents refused to take the Concorde connection substitute due to his conviction that the Concorde supersonic speeds were unnecessary, wasteful, and to be short-lived! He was right on the last count.) One of my motivations in accepting the assignment was that I would be able to take Norwegian language lessons, adding that language to the three or four I was familiar with. After my first visit to Norway, I abandoned that idea because everyone, including cab drivers, spoke better English than I would ever speak Norwegian, which sounds nothing like German, let alone the Latin languages with which I was familiar.

At the time of my assignment in Norway the population numbered about 4 million, approximately that of the greater Boston area. It is the wealthiest nation per capita in the world and regarded as the happiest. Norway's "cradle-to-grave" social support system has been reinforced greatly since its petroleum reservoirs in the North Sea were discovered and exploited, starting in 1969. However, in September 2019, the CEO of French TOTAL, the largest producer of Norwegian oil in the North Sea, started an earth-shaking shift from petroleum production to carbon storage. The void caused by declining crude production there is ideal for storing carbon emanating from fossil fuel activities. This conceptual but feasible plan, if accepted and implemented by fossil fuel industries world-wide, might provide hope that the Paris Climate Accord members' goals of attaining world-wide attenuation of the atmospheric temperatures before the end of this century may be feasible.

Four years of quarterly stewardship meetings were held in Oslo and Tromso, Norway, with nominal technical support from EXXON HQ, which I arranged. Its testing of one of the first microcomputers fabricated by the Norwegian startup, and the $20 million, was not enough to win the race. Another startup in California's Silicon Valley, headed by Steve Wozniak and Steve Jobs, called APPLE, won the microcomputer single board personal computer race.

But Esso-Europe won the oil exploration concessions in the North Sea.

26. The Legacy Lives

Fortunately, although my assignments at Corporate HQ required frequent travel to both foreign and U.S. West Coast locations, our family residence remained in New Providence. My last assignment prior to retirement in 1987 was as Manager of the Computing and Communications Department of INTERCOR in Baranquilla, Colombia, South America.

My father's health started failing him, the result of no particular illness but the implacable advance into old age. I observed his slow degeneration over a few years in the late 1970s. My mother started needing help with caring for dad at their home in Seaside/Monterey, and I made emergency trips from New Jersey to observe firsthand that mom could no longer cope with his condition. Dad could rationally converse with me, but I had to convince him to agree to a temporary stay at a first-class nursing home that could help him regain some degree of mobility by therapy and exercise. This was a remote hope and I returned to New Jersey, concerned, but hoping for the best.

My mother probably knew better but faithfully visited dad daily by public transportation. Mom had never learned to drive. Dad passed away at the nursing home September 7, 1980. I had always believed that my father would live to be 100. He was a trim muscular man but carried many unseen burdens, never complaining about his occasional bad luck or his personal betrayal by another Italian immigrant who was supposed to have been his friend and business partner in "a cinch" of a lifetime opportunity.

Three years after dad's passing I got a phone call in New Jersey from a neighbor of my mother's in Seaside, who told me that mom was wandering around during her daily walk down the hill and back from the market. I immediately arranged with a Monterey home care company to provide daily care, housekeeping, and feeding service for mom. One of the caregivers had the Friday through Sunday duty, and this lady—a Philippine lady named Elfleda Delacruz—and mom took a great liking to each other.

The in-home living assistance arrangement worked well for about two years until another call came that my mother probably needed more skilled nursing attendance than the present service could

26. The Legacy Lives

provide. While I had visited mom occasionally during the three-year period and she seemed to be doing well, this time Sandra and I flew out together and concluded that my mother needed full-time day and night nursing care. In the following two weeks we first located a supposedly first-class facility in Carmel just south of Monterey and moved mom there, listed her home for sale, conducted a garage sale, and emptied the home of everything except her clothes, personal items and photographs. There we also discovered her "secret diary," which she had kept so faithfully for those fateful four months in 1927.

During the garage sale, Elfleda and her husband, Rai, paid us a visit and admired my parents' dining room set but could not afford to purchase it. Sandra had a brilliant idea and offered the entire dining room set for nothing to Elfleda on condition that she visit mom regularly at the exclusive Carmel nursing facility to see how she was being taken care of. We returned home and again hoped for the best.

A year went by and Elfleda reported that my mother was doing very poorly. Elfleda and Rai were an exceptional couple and were recent immigrants from the Philippines. Elfleda informed us that she had just lost her regular job at the Navy Language School in Monterey due to the cessation of the Tagalog Language instruction program. She and Rai were caring for Rai's mother at their home and offered to move my mother there immediately to house, feed, and care for her as they were doing for Rai's mother. My parents' dining room set and Sandra's great idea were to yield a solution without our having to fly out for another emergency solution to mom's situation. We asked Elfleda and Rai to give us a day to consider their very kind and welcome offer. The only thing I could think of was, "What if you, Elfleda and Rai, start caring for my mother and she degenerates to the point that we need to move her back into another nursing home or hospital for which she would then not qualify due to her worsened condition?" Elfleda immediately responded, "Oh no, you do not understand, in the Philippines we do not have nursing homes, we care for our elders ourselves; she will be with us for her life as a member of our family!"

Wow. We agreed upon their fee, Elfleda and Rai moved my mother to their home and treated her for many years as a family member, restored her health and morale, and took her to their Catholic church on Sundays with the rest of their extensive family until the end. We visited mom several times in the Delacruz residence with their whole large family of sons, daughters, and grandchildren in attendance to greet and welcome us to their family and spent time with mom, who smiled a lot and looked well taken care of and happy.

26. The Legacy Lives

Eda Barbara Paredi outlived her Nino until April 4, 1999, and died at age 93. When they met on that fateful trip from New York City to Genoa in 1927, she was 21 and Nino was 29.

The entire Delacruz family of dozens by far outnumbered me, Sandra, Cat, and Jacqueline at my mother's memorial service. The Delacruz family is now involved in the medical and senior care industry in California, and Sandra and I have stayed in contact with Elfleda and Rai. We hope we will be so lucky to be in the care of people such as the Delacruzes when our time comes.

Sadly, Elfleda suffered the loss of Rai in 2019.

The American Legacy of an Italian Motorcyclist

27. Retirement

The trumpet is a demanding instrument and requires constant practice to strengthen the muscles around one's mouth, lips, and jaw—an area of the head called the "embouchure." Entering my retirement years in the late '80s I never gave a thought about hobbies other than fishing, tennis, and golf, which I had attempted to learn during the last three years of my career in Columbia. I loved fishing and tennis and hated golf.

Me, bonefish on the fly, Grand Bahamas, 2005

The American Legacy of an Italian Motorcyclist

One of my workmates at the EMCS Department, Don Robertson, was a good drummer and we always talked about his interest and continuing performance with jazz groups in New Jersey. After my retirement plus the three years of consulting, I needed a fulfilling activity, certainly not golf, to get involved in. I recalled my mom's encouragement and dug out the trumpet and devoted one to two hours a day of practice to get back my "chops." After 14 months of diligent practice I was ready to perform. I knew that Don had also retired from EXXON and was an active member and officer of the "New Jersey Jazz Society." I called him up and asked him what my options were to get back in the music business. He said, "No problem; show up every Sunday at 2 o'clock at the following locations; bring your horn and wife. Musicians are chosen on the basis of "first come, first play,"— trumpet, piano, trombone, clarinet, banjo, tuba, drums. Plenty of beer is available."

I asked Don if they played straight-ahead jazz or what? He answered, "No, man, we play Dixie-land!" I said, "You gotta be kidding! I've always dreamed about learning it but never had the opportunity; now what do I do?"

One of the NJJS members a few blocks away from our residence was also a regular Sunday participant in the jam sessions, and Don suggested I call the trombonist, Kent Blair. He suggested I buy a few Dixie-land "fakebooks," learn the tunes,

27. Retirement

and show up on Sundays. A couple of months after learning the tunes, Sandra and I started showing up to observe the protocol and eventually I was a regular participant. It was great fun; the audiences were enthusiastic. There was only one problem. After three hours of nine groups performing, if a particular member was the only one who played the clarinet, he got to play for three hours and the tunes that each of the seven-piece group would agree upon to perform would often overlap. This would result in the same tune, or tunes, being repeatedly performed: boring!

After a few months of good beer but boring repetitive tune selections, seven of us at one Sunday event agreed to form our own "traditional" jazz band, to be called the Summit Stompers Jazz Band, and to rehearse whenever possible at Kent's (he had a piano in the basement and space for seven musicians). Within a few months we started getting paying gigs, established a library of over 200 traditional jazz compositions with particular charts for each instrument, we dealt with musicians' turnover, and had a ball.

Both of our daughters, Cat and Jacqueline, after graduating from college, eventually found professional careers in the greater NYC area. The family plan was once Cat was married, Sandra and I would move south, probably to the coastal town of Savannah, Georgia. Our friends and neighbors in New Providence, NJ, were incredulous. They would question: "Why down south; don't both of your daughters work and live in the NYC area?" We would counter, "Do you know where your children will be in ten or twenty years from now?"

Me playing a gig with the Summit Stompers, 1993

We did a reality check one summer by renting a place for two weeks in the heat of July in

27. Retirement

Savannah to compare the climate to the terrible climates in Venezuela and Colombia. We determined that if the summer heat was as bad as it gets, we would have no problem. During that visit I noticed a newspaper article that highlighted a community orchestra hosted by Georgia Southern University's Armstrong Campus. The orchestra was composed of students, adult volunteers who either were or were not alumni of the university, and any other adults who were interested in performing with the orchestra. A phone number was provided to call for further information. I called and explained my musical background and interest in possibly joining the orchestra were we to move to Savannah. I was encouraged by the director to call again if we did.

In 1995, it all came together. Cat married, my father had passed away in California years before, and mom was safely cared for in Monterey. My Aunt Erma would pass away at the age of 104, and my two cousins, Elaine and Nancy, were well situated in Oakland and Auburn, California. In 1997, we sold our home in New Jersey and moved to Skidaway Island, Georgia, minutes from Savannah and Armstrong University. Before moving, we made copies of the entire library of the Summit Stompers Jazz Band, with plans to form a similar group in Savannah. In 1998, I became the head of the trumpet section of the 90-member Savannah Wind Symphony (SWINDS). I also established the Savannah Stompers Jazz Band, the replica of the Summit Stompers Jazz Band. In normal years the SWINDS performs four concerts yearly, starting with the Fall Concert and ending with the July 4th Patriotic Concert, the regularly sold-out event in the 1100-seat Fine Arts Theater. The SSJB performs for corporate events, Mardi Gras concerts, and weddings. We were hired by Disney Studios in 2009 to appear in and perform for a wedding scene in Miley Cyrus' first adult movie, *The Last Song.*

That's me to the far right

In 2010 I produced and published a CD titled *Emperor Norton's Hunch*, the title tune of the SSJB CD. The traditional jazz tune by that name is the

27. Retirement

12th and last tune on the CD. It commemorates the life and proclamations of the infamous, real, and eccentric British immigrant to San Francisco, Joshua Abraham Norton a/k/a Emperor Norton I. Lou Waters, the famous San Francisco trumpeter of the successful Yerba Buena Jazz Band of the 1940s and '50s, composed the title tune to honor the "emperor's" life. Occasionally, when we visited my parents in San Francisco, we enjoyed seeing and hearing Lou Waters in person, and he would often play *Emperor Norton's Hunch.*

CD jacket cover, published February 2010

There is no question in my mind that I would never have developed the ability to stand up before authority figures and large gatherings of employees and deliver presentations in foreign languages if it were not for the nurturing care of my parents.

The greatest regret of my dabbling in "traditional" jazz is that I was not able to produce the *Emperor Norton's Hunch* CD during my parents' lifetime. It would have made them so happy to see what my mom's natural and unanticipated musical influences had upon me. The most powerful effects of my mother's dedication and my father's encouragement were how they turned a shy little boy into a self-confident man who had a modicum of success in his professional life, a most beautiful wife, and two beautiful, successful daughters.

Me with Cat and Jacqueline, 2012

27. Retirement

Me and my beautiful wife, Sandra, in Savannah, 2015

The American Legacy of an Italian Motorcyclist

28. The Accidental Activist

On April 20, 2010, 41 miles off the Louisiana Gulf Coast, "the worst industrial accident in America's history" occurred. That Department of Justice finding referred to the Deep Water Horizon oil drilling ship, which suffered a blowout and fire, immediately killing 11 members of the drilling crew. The ship was leased by British Petroleum Corp. from Transocean Corp., whose employees aboard the vessel were responsible for the operation of the ship and the drilling activities being performed in 5100 feet of ocean depth. Beyond the ocean bottom the well was drilled to a depth of 18,360 feet (about 3-1/2 miles). It was in the final stage of being carefully abandoned by an injection of specially prepared cement in and around the bottom hole by Halliburton Corp. Within 48 hours of the blowout, the entire vessel and large-diameter riser pipe connecting it to the wellhead and blowout preventer on the ocean bottom capsized, leaving the well fluid gushing uncontrollably until September 19, 2010. The well was finally sealed by Wild Well Corporation, which was belatedly contracted to properly abandon the well after several failed attempts by the partnership. There was nothing in the world "off the shelf" available to deploy during the months of the blowout. The partnership's efforts to design and construct a number of ad-hoc devices were abject failures. The DOJ trial also concluded that the accident was caused by "deliberate misconduct and gross negligence."

It was only estimated—conservatively—that four million barrels of crude oil leaked to the ocean during the five months of uncontrollable flow of the blowout. The U.S. Coast Guard was only able to monitor uncounted numbers of dead birds of 102 species. In addition, the corpses of 6,165 sea turtles and 25,000 dolphins and whales were counted. Marine scientists determined that a sea bottom area the size of Oklahoma had been rendered permanently devoid of organic life. The villain was a surfactant called COREXIT, hastily approved by the Coast Guard to be applied to many square miles of ocean surface to hide and sink vast crude-oil slicks. The surfactant was later determined by scientists to be 52 times more lethal to micro-organisms than crude oil droplets.

I became transfixed by the press, TV, and radio reports for the remainder of 2010, which seemed never to go beyond what was being reported to the newspapers. Few reporters seemed to pursue anything more than what they believed to interest the typical reader. I contacted a close friend of mine, Hank Appen, then retired in Florida, who had risen to a top position in Esso-Columbia. Hank gave me some tips on discoveries relating to the incident that were starting to appear in the monthly *Oil & Gas Journal*. Before the litigation of the catastrophe started, I prepared and made presentations about the disaster to a number of Savannah chapters of Kiwanis, the Rotary Club, the Audubon Society, public libraries, and similar organizations using PowerPoint and viewgraphs.

About 1-1/2 years after the blowout was controlled and the well abandoned, the litigation process concluded. The astonishing result was that the party of BP, Transocean, and Halliburton was fined $66 *billion* for its managerial misconduct in the Macondo (official name of the federal concession) incident. The defendants' shares of the fines were, respectively, BP, $44 billion; Transocean, $20 billion; and Halliburton, $2 billion.

During this time, I wrote a series of more than a dozen letters to the editor of *The Savannah Morning News*. The letters' purpose was to inform the public in layman's terms how normal operating practices in petroleum operations can degenerate into catastrophic environmental damage and/or fatalities of operations staff. The Obama administration soon discovered that *no federal organization existed to oversee the activities of the oil and gas industry.* There were no operational standards to prevent major accidents or hold "Big Oil" responsible for environmental accidents that caused damage to state, federal and private properties, or presented hazards to life and limb of private citizens and private industry. The long-established Department of the Interior was finally charged to create the Bureau of Offshore Energy and Management (BOEM), which in turn established the Bureau of Safety and Environmental Enforcement (BSEE). The latter's mission statement clearly stipulates that it was to *develop and administer the enforcement of new safety standards* covering a range of operational practices commonly executed in the drilling activities of the oil industry.

Six hundred new federal employees were recruited to staff the new department. The BSEE immediately set to work and eventually started drafting and publishing proposed regulations in the Federal Register, an online list available to the public and industry, including the American Petroleum Industry (API). The API is believed to be the most wealthy and influential lobbying body in the world, composed of all major American oil corporations.

An example of how the system works can be illustrated by examining the critically important piece of equipment, used in *all* drilling operations, called the blowout preventer (BOP). Its failure to prevent the blowout of BP's Deepwater Horizon's leased drillship from Transocean was a major subject of investigation and litigation. For six years after the "worst industrial accident in U.S. history" there were six proposed BSEE-originated drafts of safety standards listed in the register, some of which dealt with dozens of aspects of the use, control, and testing of BOPs. As soon as any one of these proposed BSEE drafts was issued, the API members from any and all of the oil "majors or minors" would immediately search for the "poisoned" words such as "must," "required," "enforced," "mandatory," etc. The three-month review period on the offending statement in the Federal Register would be extended for further review, particularly by the API, until the BSEE would relent and soften the wording. The most critical object in the API review process became, and continues to be, the BOP. By comparison, the least complex BOPs, by today's standards, were installed on every workover or drilling rig on Lake Maracaibo and were required by the Creole Corporation to be tested at the beginning of every shift. All operations from "making hole" (drilling) to running and setting casing, installing down-hole devices, changing a worn-out drill-bit, had to be stopped to allow the crew-chief to test the BOP's operation. Within a few years of the founding of the BSEE, the API established a simple test to determine whether any proposed rule, even if pertaining to the BOP, was to be rejected if it was "excessively expensive or inconvenient." The BSEE soon became ridiculed by other regulatory agencies within the government and organizations beyond the government concerned with environmental issues.

On December 14, 2018, I received a phone call from David Hilzenrath, who identified himself as a Washington, D.C., journalist with a nonprofit organization called the Project on Governmental Oversight (POGO). As an investigative reporter for *The Washington Post*, he had reported upon the Deepwater Horizon BP disaster and had actually been present at the DOJ hearing, which resulted in the $66 billion fine of the three defendants. That trial started about 1-1/2 years after I had completed my study of the accident and had made several presentations on the disaster. At the trial's conclusion and after joining POGO, David wrote a three-part study of how BP and other big oil firms continued to thwart the efforts of the BSEE in issuing enforceable safety procedures in the petroleum drilling sector. The first part was "All Hell Breaks Loose," the second part was "Rollback," the third was "Big Oil Rules."

Before continuing the call from David, I asked him how he had tracked me down. He said that POGO had a computer application that searched every U.S. newspaper's letters-to-the-editor section daily

28. The Accidental Activist

to identify letters on topics of interest to its reporters. *The Savannah Morning News* requires letters authors to provide their name, address, and phone number as a condition for publication. (Kudos to all newspapers for having the requirement, and to POGO for having and applying this search tool.)

David then asked me to bring his report up on my computer and go to a particular chapter, paragraph, and sentence to offer my reaction to his conclusion or statement. I never had to take any exception to his analysis or particular conclusions. In one particular instance, however, I was able to share with him something dramatic in support of a BOP-related conclusion he had made that added considerable credibility to his report: Cameron Valves Corp. merged with Schlumberger Oilfield Services in August 2016, six years after the Deepwater Horizon accident. Cameron remains the "gold standard" in oilfield valve and BOP design and construction. It was Cameron that supplied the BOP in the Deepwater Horizon calamity. A fortuitous coincidence occurred during the installation of the BOP by Transocean workers being observed by Cameron technicians. That observation was recorded and presented at the trial; it absolved Cameron of any complicity, guilt, or malfeasance, and prevented the company from being an additional defendant in the litigation. Indeed, how was that possible since it was determined that the BOP had failed to prevent the blowout? The Cameron BOP was being installed atop the wellhead on the deck of the Deepwater Horizon prior to its lowering to the ocean bottom. Cameron technicians observed Transocean technicians altering part of the electronic circuitry within the control modules of the BOP and protested: What were the Transocean employees doing and why? The Transocean technicians defended their actions, and the Cameron reps made a note of the event, which was presented during the trial. The BOP was salvaged by Wild Well Corp. after the well was properly abandoned and the BOP sent for analysis, but no judgment could be made that a particular component or bit of control code in the BOP module was a factor or cause of the BOP's failure.

What I had discovered in my study of the Macondo BP event was that at an international symposium held in London several years prior to the accident, Cameron's head engineering design executive had made a presentation addressing the growing complexity of BOP design. The conclusion of his technical presentation was that "the petroleum industry has added to its BOP performance criteria new and sophisticated autonomous BOP functionality, compromising their reliability." The words here are mine paraphrasing much engineering jargon. BOPs had inadvertently become less safe by *design*. And this was the state

28. The Accidental Activist

of BOP safety four or five years before the Deepwater Horizon failure. Jumping forward to 2020 and we read and heard that the U.S. Federal DOI/BOEM/BSEE cabinet-level agencies had been directed by our chief executive in the second quarter of 2020 to relax many safety standards, so as to be more responsive to the API and the oil industry. Anyone interested in keeping up-to-date on such matters would be well served to look up POGO on the internet. Mr. Hilzenrath continues to probe current government developments in the regulatory field over many branches of industry and related government departments.

Another fortuitous incident reinforcing my accidental activism was precipitated by my first of 15 letters to *The Savannah Morning News*. This letter was published on Friday, August 24, 2018. The very next day, Saturday, August 25, the SMN front page Section 1 contained a photograph of a young lady, Paulita Bennett-Martin, and several columns "above the fold" about her. Ms. Bennett-Martin had been recently appointed to a position with OCEANA, the worldwide ocean protection nonprofit organization. I turned to my wife, Sandra, at the breakfast table and said, "Holy smoke, look at this; I gotta find out tomorrow how to get hold of this lady!" I found an OCEANA phone number on Monday, dialed it, and a woman's voice answered. I introduced myself and asked to speak to Ms. Paulita Bennett-Martin, whose title is "campaign organizer." The voice answered, "Wait, are you the person who wrote that letter to the SMN last Friday? I made a note to try and find you today." The die was cast. I continued writing many more letters to the SMN and attended local community functions that Paulita was organizing to gain Georgia coast-wide support for OCEANA events. Paulita was particularly successful in mobilizing a wide range of stakeholders to oppose petroleum exploration and drilling off the Georgia coast. We arranged joint presentations to the same local organizations I had made presentations to years prior on the BP debacle and a few additional organizations.

28. The Accidental Activist

Me with Paulita Bennett-Martin of OCEANA

In November of 2019, Paulita arranged for me to join dozens of other OCEANA delegates from West Coast and East Coast states on an OCEANA "fly-in" to Washington, D.C., to meet with members of Congress and their staffs in small groups of three to five of us, focused on particular states' congressional representatives. The final day a larger group of us met with the Secretary of the BOEM and senior staff to hear how they were prepared to issue and manage seismic exploration licenses to several European companies to initiate months of seismic exploration up and down the East Coast in federal waters. As a result of OCEANA's diligent and purposeful pursuit to prevent, or at least forestall, the unnecessary and destructive seismic and exploratory drilling program, a federal circuit court judge came to the rescue. The South Carolina judge had issued a 30-day "stay," that, successively issued, was successful in forestalling the initiation of those seismic research projects. Such projects would have affected every Atlantic coast state's waters beyond its state's three-mile border to 200 miles at the international ocean water boundary.

Another amazing, reliable, comprehensive source of research and long-term studies of the effects of the petroleum industry worldwide came to my attention in mid-2019. One afternoon, a discussion aired on NPR between Terry Grosz and Rachel

Maddow about Maddow's new book *BLOWOUT* stopped me in my tracks. The following day I went straight to our local Barnes & Noble bookstore and was approached by the receptionist, who asked me what I was looking for. When I asked if *BLOWOUT* was in stock, she told me it was flying off the shelves. *BLOWOUT* is a cover-to-cover read on the economic, societal, industrial, and political effects of the "richest, most destructive industry on earth." The chapter on "subsidence" really caught my attention, because it relates to experiences I confronted during my professional life. Subsidence is an important phenomenon that offends my environmental sensibilities: turns out that the earth sinks in localities because of petroleum and gas extraction and the geographical proximity to "low countries" in and within various locations of the world.

In the first seven years of my petroleum engineering profession, my young family and I lived on the eastern shore of Lake Maracaibo, Venezuela. The flagpole at the center of the parking lot of our headquarters had, in addition to the flag of Venezuela, a strip of colored tape stuck to a point of the pole about 12 feet above the pavement. I soon learned that the tape marked the height of the lake surface within 50 yards westward that was being held back by the six-foot high dike that ran for a distance of approximately 40 miles northward and similarly southward of the parking

28. The Accidental Activist

lot. We lived on the eastern shore of the lake, with lowlands that extended hundreds of miles eastward toward the drainage flatland of the Orinoco River basin, which was laced by the zig-zagging courses of numerous smaller rivers, all of them winding their way downstream to the South Atlantic Ocean. The construction and maintenance of our dike was supported by the two or three principal foreign petroleum corporations whose producing fields dipped westward under the lake and rose upward to the east. My company's oil reservoirs were all below the lake bottom.

The subsidence we observed over time was caused by the daily withdrawal of millions of barrels from the more than 4000 oil wells and billions of cubic feet of gas. All those many years of withdrawals, starting from the discovery of the first deposits, followed by numerous later discoveries that reached the development stage, had literally been supporting the overlying earth.

Until about 15 to 20 years ago, the state of Oklahoma had never in living memory seen or felt a small earthquake. Then earthquakes started to occur all over the flatlands of Oklahoma. The Oklahomans started wondering if the rapidly growing new gas well drilling technique called "fracking" had anything to do with the earthquakes. The public was questioning the possibility of a cause (fracking) with the effect (earthquakes), which the fracking industry ridiculed outright. The fracking industry provided significant labor opportunities. Maddow's book describes the building anxiety between rural communities and ranchers starting to observe pollution of the previously plentiful potable water wells that met their farming, livestock, and homestead requirements. The water smelled bad, tasted awful, was undrinkable, and, in some cases, was accompanied by gas flowing from their taps. Scientists, particularly geologists, were drawn into the cause-and-effect issue and either dismissed the theory due to insufficient evidence or fear of public pressure from either side of the believers or non-believers.

Maddow's retelling is great reading that follows the patient efforts of one highly respected local geologist in Oklahoma. He eventually collected sufficient data to support his research and data collection, which established the positive correlation of subsidence to Oklahoma's earthquakes and water pollution. Farmers and ranchers who counted on the formerly pristine freshwater aquifers were suffering. At the time of this writing, market forces have caused a dramatic lowering of prices for natural gas, which has appreciably reduced the demand for "tight shale, fracked gas." Tighter state controls over how retrieved fracking fluids must be collected and disposed of and the growth of solar and wind—so-called clean and renewable energy sources—are all on a growth path. *BLOWOUT* and its revelations and conclusions are supported by an impressive list of bibliographic references underpinning Maddow's entertaining but sobering narrative.

One state in particular, New York, having observed the environmental damage suffered by Oklahoma, has simply outlawed the fracking industry's plans to introduce it in the state. Other upper midwest states have proven reserves of natural gas in similar tight-shale formations. But even the API acknowledges that the U.S. has proven reserves in existing domestic crude and gas reservoirs to meet its demands for 100 years at present market requirements; every year conventional drilling methods add to replace what was consumed. Those proven annual reserves will probably be maintained at close to 100 years' supply.

The U.S. petroleum industry is critically important in furnishing essential and reliable domestic supplies of high-energy, petroleum-derived fuel for many years to come for our country's military and civil aviation needs. EXXON made various short-term investments in the 1980s in non-petroleum-related industries such as peripheral computer development, replacement of spent uranium nuclear fuel tube assemblies, graphite tubular manufacturers, and other start-up ventures. I was assigned to EXXON Enterprises late in its limited life to close down its computer operations units.

A particular resource in America's energy sector is "The Grid," the high-voltage electrical distribution network that has been called the largest interconnected machine on earth. "The Grid" was initiated in the post-WWII years and comprises 200,000 miles of high-voltage electrical transmission lines and 5.5 million miles of local lower-voltage distribution lines. It connects thousands of electrical generating plants to factories, homes, and businesses. Unfortunately, it is also considered to be obsolescent and concentrated in our eastern and western industrialized regions and Texas, and is largely or entirely absent in the less industrialized and rural areas of the U.S.

In January 2020, the Energy Department of the Pacific Northwest National Laboratory published a study that concluded that a full-scale "smart grid" could be developed and working by 2030 that would reduce annual carbon emissions from the electric power sector by 442 metric tons, representing 12% of its present capacity and the equivalent of 66 coal-fired power plants. Thousands of miles of new transmission lines would be needed to connect more clean energy sources to electrically powered demand centers. The present power grid cannot support a massive shift to low carbon power (clean energy) sources needed to avoid catastrophic climate change impacts. Such phenomena are presently apparent in the U.S. Gulf Coast, with intensifying hurricane seasons, and are increasing the severity of the West Coast's cataclysmic forest fires.

The catastrophic failure of the Texas' electrical power grid in February 2021 attracted the word's attention. Investigation of the "Electric Reliability Council of Texas" (ERCOT) in this industrial disaster was immediately started before the widespread effects—including many fatalities in private residences, including children—were known. The state electric grid's failure had previously occurred in 2011, prompting detailed analyses that called for major operating and maintenance corrections to electrical equipment at 650 independent electrical-power-generating plants. The natural gas suppliers' equipment froze and failed. Four-and-a-half million customers of the ERCOT grid were affected in the 2011 incident. The 1935 Federal Power Act had been given the authority to regulate power companies that engage in interstate commerce. Apparently, the secessionist attitudes of many Texans led the state to establish its own electrical grid to avoid influence and federal oversight by the Federal Energy Regulatory Commission. At that, there are two remote areas of Texas which must rely on connections to the Mexican power grid and the Panhandle area being connected to the western U.S. grid. Electrical energy shortages resulting from these radical inclement weather events caused ERCOT to consider rationing supply by rotating outages. Wind and solar sources of the Texas electrical supply account for 25% of Texas' electrical requirements. A long-term solution could be the accelerated growth of Texas' renewable energy supplies in those vast open spaces of the state and those of its northern neighbors.

The total absence of today's grid in parts of the U.S. interior prevents the large-scale development of clean and renewable sources of private and municipal solar and wind "farms." Investment in modernizing and expanding the grid's coverage in such areas could provide for large new labor requirements for their reconstruction and expansion and, most importantly, for the following private or state investment in clean energy development and solar and wind farms. Proximate locations of a wider, more secure "smart" grid, employing advanced computer technology, would provide closer and cheaper connection points to supplies of new sources of renewable electric energy. In turn, new industrial growth in previously exclusively rural communities of those affected states would nurture new industries requiring additional labor. Those low cost and replaceable clean energy supplies would result in local labor opportunities for local new industries, creating goods for regional, domestic or worldwide markets. That function is exactly what the present but obsolescent and limited grid performs by connecting the electrical power sources to the demand for electrical energy, including all manner of commercial industries staffed by local labor.

In recent years the topic of American infrastructure degradation has drawn much attention and the prime example has been the complex of U.S. bridges urgently requiring substantial and critical repair to avoid collapses, causing significant fatalities. The recent spate of West Coast electric utilities' high-tension electrical cables collapsing from falling wind-driven timber debris igniting widespread forest fires has been a significant cause of recent calamitous California-wide forest fires. The "dumb and obsolescent" present grid should lead the list of the U.S. infrastructure demanding immediate action.

Global warming phenomena leading to climate change in all regions of the world is well documented and understood by the scientific community. The international importance of these phenomena culminated in the establishment of the Paris Climate Accord by 195 countries, including the U.S, in 2015. After considerable research, the PCA adopted the common goal of attenuating the increase in temperature of the earth's atmosphere by the year 2100 to 3.6° F (2° C) of present temperature.

The great weakness in the PCA is the complete absence of any enforcement measures. The science supporting its conclusions is unassailable. But the fact is that a significant majority of its members have not the means to adopt control measures to immediately start addressing the implications of the quantifiable objectives. For example, how can the poorest countries afford to adopt and install expensive stack emission scrubbers which exist in the U.S. but are not even employed by our dirty fuel-driven electrical generating industries due to the devices "excessive cost, high maintenance requirements." Indeed, the U.S. federal government itself has recently attempted to oppose California's automotive fuel efficiency standards as they apply to new vehicles. India's economy is significantly dependent on its coal industry for all sectors of its energy needs and has a substantial labor sector of coal miners who depend upon coal mining for stable jobs. How are "fair shares" of capital investments by the PCA members to be calculated for their investments in clean energy-based new facilities? Are the wealthiest members to carry the entire burden of cleaning up their energy sources while the poorest members do little or nothing? A sizable coal-export industry by Australia accounts for a substantial financial component of its exports. Its interior is a prime source of potential income from new wind and solar energy farms similar to the interior of the U.S. Does Australia have a domestic market for such inexpensive clean electrical energy?

Avoidance and hostility of any government to consider and support alternative clean and renewable energy sources is to deny the scientific community's evidence supporting the conclusion that ocean warming causes climate change. The withdrawal by the U.S. from the Paris Climate Accord on Nov. 4, 2020, signaled to the other 195 members of the Accord that the U.S. discredits the scientific community. We and the rest of the world must not accept increasing global warming and its consequences. Fortunately, the new U.S. Administration in early 2021 announced to the world its intention to rejoin the PCA. This was universally welcomed by all the members of the PCA.

There is an argument based upon who and what has been credited for inventing the alternative to whale oil for illumination and engines to replace horse-drawn vehicles. Commercially useful petroleum was discovered in Pennsylvania by America's "Colonel Drake" after our Civil War. The first internal combustion engines were invented in 1876 by Nicolaus Otto, Gottlieb Daimler, and Wilhelm Maybach, and patented in Germany. Henry Ford invented mass production in America by moving an electrically powered "assembly line" past specialized teams of laborers stationed at points along the way to assemble thousands of low-cost Ford Model A's and T's, which flooded the market and the roads. The industrial revolution was launched all over the world, and the world was never the same. Fast forward to today, and we have "corrupted democracy, rogue state Russia, and the richest, most destructive industry on earth," according to Rachel Maddow's difficult-to-deny conclusions spelled out in *BLOWOUT*.

All this wealth concentrated in the petroleum industry spawned vast networks of refineries, producing fuels and plastics of all manner. The latter are essentially un-recyclable and are infecting our earth and seas. Those industries should lead the effort to clean it up. They have the most power, money, and technical acumen to lead the cleanup. The PCA, composed of 195 members, from major democracies to despotic governments and poor, undeveloped rural-based economies, seems to be assuming that those responsible for having ruined the seas and atmosphere should step up and lead a recovery effort. We cannot wait until 2099 to suddenly apply a planet-wide reduction of atmospheric and ocean temperatures. An international multi-disciplinary organization of scientists and executives from select energy sectors and academia, not all from the petrochemical sector, must be established *now* to develop and execute an action plan. Annual incremental and measurable metrics must demonstrate that progress is being made in the remaining decades years of this century. Funding of the effort must be derived from various sectors, governmental and industrial, and particularly from the worldwide petroleum industries. There should be a role to play by the United Nations and the PCA to ensure that smaller, poorer nations' interests are sought and considered.

At this writing many things are in a state of flux at all levels of our government. Many federal-level departments will be affected in 2021, since those cabinet-level units have been bent for four years to loosen environmental protection measures, ignore alternative energy sources, avoid addressing international anxieties, and movements to address global and ocean warming phenomena.

The American Legacy of an Italian Motorcyclist

29. Devil's Bargain

I wrote this account of my parents' lives and mine at the urging of our two daughters. They have known about some, but not all, of the experiences recounted in this book. I had put off writing my parents' stories because I was convinced our daughters had heard them all. I now realize I was wrong about that. Having written this account of my parents' lives, I realize how fortunate I was to learn from them, to unthinkingly apply their experiences and ethics and judgment at points in my life where I might have followed my own intuition. They were both in uncharted territories at different times in their lives but weathered all the obstacles that arose, most of which were beyond their control. World wars and national cultural or economic reversals seemed to pop up in their paths at critical junctures. Upon their marriage, only four months after their meeting as total strangers on a steamship crossing the

Atlantic, they dove into marriage in between two world wars. Had they chosen to remain in Italy in the comfortable surroundings of a beautiful town and a successful, industrious, and educated family, I would have been born there and would likely have become involved in Mussolini's fascist dream as a youthful victim, like my Italian Uncle Maso, who barely survived in WWII.

And what good fortune it was for my parents to wind up in beauteous, cosmopolitan, and immigrant-friendly San Francisco, where I was born in 1932. San Francisco had not only survived the deadly earthquake and fire of 1906 but, by 1915, a mere nine years later, presented the world with the spectacular, never-to-be-equaled Panama Pacific International Exposition, erasing its image as an uncultured town inhospitable to immigrants.

Lastly, I found it impossible for me in writing this account to separate my parents' lives from mine, even after their deaths. Their lives seem to have lived on in mine throughout my corporate career and even in my life after retirement.

If I am able to influence a few readers by this account of my parents' and my life's experiences, then I will conclude that my book was much more valuable than the time and effort expended in its production. I have had the opportunity to understand the inner workings of the most influential industrial complex in the world and its

29. Devil's Bargain

modern-day deliberate damage to humanity and to the future health of our planet writ large.

The year 2020 witnessed the confluence of so many "natural" disasters that even a partial list is alarming: from Covid-19 to record-setting rainfall in specific areas of prior drought; of California wildfires so intense, so widespread, and so much earlier than normal seasons; large ships finding their way to the North Pole unencumbered by sea ice; the measurable increase in sea surface temperatures; the degradation of the extent and quality of coral reefs; grains of plastic garbage appearing in the intestines and flesh of sea life...and the list goes on.

In spite of such evidence, much of the public does not comprehend that these are not passing phenomena but the unavoidable price some of us must pay to enjoy the privilege of living in the modern world. This is a devil's bargain, and science and its new discoveries must not only be accepted but sped up dramatically to figure out new and profitable means of recycling and inventing substitutes for plastic packaging. Just as whale oil was eliminated as a fuel source for lamps by the discovery of petroleum's first derivative, kerosene, clean and renewable fuel sources must replace energy required from internal combustion engines. Vast amounts of clean and renewable energy (read solar and wind) exist to produce electric power in the U.S. The obsolescent "high-voltage grid" must be modernized by government initiatives, corporate backing, and public support.

All this having been said, for a long time to come there will be a need for the oil industry to provide fuel for commercial and military aviation. The fact that the U.S. has proven reserves of 100 years at present annual consumption rates and every recent year it has maintained that reserve by newly found domestic resources seems to assure that the domestically driven market for clean and renewable energy resources should be aggressively supported by our government, not suppressed.

Devices to clean "smokestack" emissions to prevent the compounds that are released to the atmosphere leading to ocean warming have been available for a long time. Their widespread industrial use has been avoided because they are expensive or inconvenient. Why are there not more funds available to university or federal agencies to research and develop technologies to directly support R&D programs to decrease or eliminate the global warming and sea water warming phenomena already affecting sea life? Politically driven movements popular with younger generation voters such as the "green new deal," elicit more ridicule than support. The increased appreciation and application of science in all fields must be supported or our long-term future as an intelligent life-form on this planet will be threatened.

30. Venezuela's Coda

Recent news reports have disclosed the deplorable decline and probably moribund status of the Venezuelan petroleum industry. A combination of various factors has reduced one of the world's primary sources of sizable and steady petroleum supplies to a nation that barely can provide gasoline to its civilian automobile and motor transport market. Its vast mechanical petroleum infrastructure has deteriorated to such a degree that its coastal waters are being polluted by constant and increasing crude oil slicks emanating from Lake Maracaibo. In 1960, Venezuela was one of the five countries that founded the Organization of Petroleum Exporting Countries. OPEC is the international cartel formed to coordinate petroleum policies of its members and provide technology and aid to its members in developing their petroleum industries. To this day, Venezuela has the largest proven oil reserves in the world, with 300 *trillion* barrels as of 2016, resulting in 1,374 years of domestic national consumption. The EXXON Venezuelan subsidiary I started to work for in the late 1950s could outproduce ARAMCO of Saudi Arabia at a rate of 4 million BPD if called for by our Venezuelan refineries. The ongoing pandemic presently in late 2020 has resulted in a dramatic lowering of demand by the worldwide transportation sector. Crude oil prices today in late 2020 are approximately $40 per barrel and would be lower if Saudi Arabia and Russia had not joined to hold their crude prices at higher levels.

There are multiple causes for the state of Venezuela's petroleum industry's collapse. The first has been its inability to preserve its brief history of democratically run national governance, which started in the 1957. That year marked a popular uprising centered in Caracas, resulting in the overthrow of an almost 30-year dictatorship and the beginning of a close to 10-year period of governance by peaceful, democratically leaning parties. Nonetheless, the inception and development of the Venezuelan petroleum industry started just before that period in which the American Rockefeller family made the earliest massive investments in the rural, commercial, and petroleum sectors. Early in the 1970s the exclusively foreign petroleum corporations such as EXXON, Shell, Gulf etc., decided to initiate a period of withdrawal from Venezuela by gradually

30. Venezuela's Coda

and prematurely returning their 30-year petroleum concession holdings to the Venezuelan government as all concessions would be starting to lapse. The reasons for this withdrawal were many, but the primary incentive was spurred by the success of OPEC in coordinating its worldwide influence on petroleum prices. For several years thereafter EXXON netted as much income by furnishing "technical support" to the Venezuelan National entity "PDVSA" (Venezuelan Petroleum Inc.) as it did prior to the nationalization of the industry.

Then entered the Venezuelan predilection for the beginning of a return to military dictators. Cesar Chavez, a Venezuelan army senior officer, tried an overthrow of the government in 1998. Chavez was a well-schooled young man who grew to be a dedicated reformist and admirer of venerated South American figures, from Simon Bolivar, "El Libertador," to Cuba's contemporary leaders. Chavez's "Bolivarian Revolutionary Army" launched a failed attempt in 1992 to overthrow the government. He was arrested and imprisoned for two years but was freed as a result of his senior military supporters bringing pressure to bear on the government. He was subsequently elected to his first presidential term in February 1999 and effected constitutional reform by January 2001. His second term started in January that year and culminated in January 2007. It was marked by an active opposition, a failed coup attempt, strikes, and a recall referendum that failed. His third presidential term from January 2007 to January 2013, and his fourth term ran from then to March 2013. He died in March 2013, age 58, in Caracas. His political ideology ran from "Bolivarianism" to Marxism and invented conspiracy theories. All the while he was supported by a growing cabal of senior Venezuelan military officers. He wound up appointing a total of 1200 military generals whose families continue to enjoy lavish lifestyles while decimating the professional ranks within the PDVSA of well-educated HQ staff and petroleum field executives and staff, mostly expat foreigners. The senior staff at HQ and field operations are political appointees who had no previous experience in petroleum operations, most critically in the maintenance field.

The slow and irreversible degeneration of the vast mechanical infrastructure in the Lake Maracaibo oilfields continues under the administration of Chavez's successor, Maduro. He was Chavez's hand-picked successor prior to Chavez's death in 2013. Maduro, a bus driver, became Chavez's trusted driver in the later Chavez years. While all this political and social chaos was underway, the sole source of Venezuela's industry and foreign trade income was petroleum. To reduce the expense of the PDVSA oilfield operations management, high- and mid-level professional positions were eliminated in Caracas and

30. Venezuela's Coda

Maracaibo. The slow but implacable physical deterioration of the huge operational machinery, tank farms, and thousands of miles of submarine pipelines at the bottom of saltwater Lake Maracaibo, filled with crude oil, continues. Even if not being pumped, crude oil remains there and continues to pollute shorelines beyond the Lake.

The Venezuelan treasury has no capability to restore PDVSA's maintenance budget. There will be no foreign interest of its "Big Oil" corporations to dream of re-entering and rebuilding the moribund infrastructure of the Lake Maracaibo oil operation's mechanical complex of pipelines, scores of production platforms, and gas collection, recompression and injection platforms the size of football fields. Most of this infrastructure is idle, inoperable, but still sitting out there on the lake and leaking. It is impossible to prevent or remedy this continuing deterioration of the gigantic infrastructure of oilfield operation that took 75 years to build. The primary source of Venezuela's vaunted "greatest proven petroleum reserves in the world" are its eastern Venezuelan "tar-sands" deposits. These are vast open-air surface- to moderate-depth deposits of tar-soaked sand. Such "reserves" are identical to Canadian tar-sand deposits in its south-western sector. The only way to recover such low-grade petroleum is to dilute it with expensive solvents to render it pumpable. With the foreseeable midterm low value of crude oil and the ongoing market-driven development of clean and renewable energy almost worldwide, Venezuela's future looks very dim and its oil industry will likely die.

Letters to the Editor

The American Legacy of an Italian Motorcyclist

1. MYTHS OF GEORGIA'S COASTLINE

—Robert Paredi, August 21, 2018

Georgia's coastline measures 100 miles. The petroleum industry's exploration, drilling and development would have no impact on Georgia's adjacent coastlines' contamination by crude oil. These are the two myths.

The first statement above is misleading and based on the straight-line distance from Savannah, the northern border with South Carolina, to St. Mary's, the southern coastal border to Florida, measures only 100 miles of Atlantic Ocean frontage. The *actual,* never-measured salt water frontage, including tidally exposed river banks, comprises homes, tourist facilities, marinas, industries, and commercial fishing bases. All such facilities and more would be affected by any petroleum-contaminated waters twice a day at high tides. The

The American Legacy of an Italian Motorcyclist

Georgia coast tides, as any fisherman, beach-goer, or coastal property owner will tell you, range from 6 to 9 feet above low tide twice daily, not counting extremes caused by occasional northeast storms and exceptionally destructive hurricanes. Coastal Georgia's unique tidal phenomenon is the result of the Georgia Bight, as every coastal map demonstrates. So, the actual tide-affected salt water frontages of Georgia are anybody's guess, and probably comprise many multiples of the 100-mile commonly stated distance. All tidally affected miles of major Georgia riverbanks occupied by residences, industries, and tourist facilities must be included in the real distance of tide-affected waterfronts.

The second myth is propagated by the petroleum industry. That is, an ocean-based exploration project would have no negative impact upon an adjacent coastline. Actually, the exploration phase is the most dangerous and expensive phase of all petroleum resource development. Recall British Petroleum's catastrophic project in 2010 off the Louisiana coast, leading to the sudden loss of thousands of feet of control casing and electrical cable connected to a stack of safety valves on the ocean bottom. This was a human error-caused debacle costing 11 lives, months of failed attempts to stop thousands of barrels a day of crude oil from fouling hundreds of square miles of ocean habitat and hundreds of miles of coastline, and billions of

1. MYTHS OF GEORGIA'S COASTLINE

dollars of equipment loss and fines; the latter continue to be paid to Louisiana claimants and the federal government. Louisiana's commercial and tourist fishery activities continue to be affected.

I am a retired petroleum engineer and have studied the effects related above during my career. I urge all stakeholders potentially affected by proposed Georgia offshore petroleum exploration and development to instigate and support authoritative studies to protect Georgia from the scourge of such activity.

Update to Letter #1:

In September 2018 I thought to investigate the possibility that an oceanographer might have studied the popularly stated "100-mile oceanfront of Georgia" to determine the true frontage rather than the easily measured straight-line distance from South Carolina to Florida, the so-called "crow's flight" miles. The Skidaway Institute of Oceanography is an extension of the University of Georgia located a few miles from our residence. I visited the SKIO and mentioned my curiosity to Dr. Mike Sullivan, the head SKIO scientist, who referred me to Dr. Clark Alexander, who had indeed done a study on the subject. Dr. Alexander was pleased to meet with me and share his findings, which had been published a few years earlier. His study concluded that the measured distance of the ocean frontage was 1,110 miles. More importantly, the study was limited by the funds of the grant to two GA westward highways: GA Route 17 and U.S. Highway 95, which are primary roads connecting Atlantic Ocean-bordering states, from Maine to Florida. Numerous large GA rivers extend far westward beyond the many rivers' highway bridges. Also excluded from his study were the perimeters of 16 offshore GA islands, the majority of which include extensive shorelines from major resorts, commercial properties, and private homes and homeowners associations. Upon my question to Dr. Alexander, "How many miles of high tide-affected river and island shores been included in your study and added to the 1,110 miles of the grant-limited study, what might have been the real number?" Dr. Alexander rubbed his chin and said, "Thousands of more miles."

2. "FINDING OUT" MEANS DRILLING

—Robert Paredi, October 17, 2018

Regarding the SMN question to Georgia's District 1 U.S. Congressman (R) Buddy Carter about his position on offshore Georgia petroleum exploration, Carter clearly said he wants to "find out if there is any oil there." My degree is in petroleum engineering, and my whole career was with the largest American oil corporation. Years were spent in the field working with geologists determining where to drill wells. There is no way to determine whether an underground geologic structure may contain oil, gas, or water solely by seismic and gravimetric procedures. Drilling is essential.

Unfortunately, there is a vast difference between drilling "exploration" wells versus "development" wells. Exploration wells take months to drill, while the latter sometimes take only days. Exploration wells are immeasurably more dangerous, prone to human error, flawed management, and imperfect drilling crew performance and/or training. Most alarmingly, undue and unwarranted reliance is placed upon a complex mechanical device, the "Blowout Preventer" (BOP).

The evolution in design, testing, performance, and the cost of the BOP has risen exponentially as the practice of drilling below the ocean floor to depths of miles has evolved. The BOP had always been a relatively simple device in terrestrial or shallow water operations. However, the Chief Design & Development Engineer of Cameron Corp., which designs and builds BOPs, revealed in 2006 that the additional complexity in design and manufacture of the BOP have not improved its reliability.

The BOP unfortunately has allowed drilling operators to assume as a last resort, if a "loss of well control" occurs in the drilling process, one can always count on the BOP operating properly to avoid catastrophe. The "worst industrial accident in American history," was the BP Macondo exploration drilling accident in the Gulf of Mexico, 21 miles off the Louisiana coast in 2010, which cost the lives of 11 drilling crew members and over $65 billion in fines. It was declared by the DOJ to have been caused by "deliberate misconduct and gross negligence" of several parties. A number of mistakes had already made by the drilling crew. However, the tragic demand by the client's

2. "FINDING OUT" MEANS DRILLING

unqualified senior BP official remonstrating with the Transocean operations manager was: "What's the problem; you've got a BOP haven't you?" The Transocean contractor yielded to the BP exec's objective of saving a few days of almost a $1B a day in rig lease fees. The BOP failed when needed.

Eleven lives and more than $65B later, such risks persist in the industry.

The American Legacy of an Italian Motorcyclist

3. ATTACK ON GEORGIA'S COAST

—Robert Paredi, December 13, 2018

America's seniors recall what Pearl Harbor Day, Dec. 7, 1941, signifies. Dec 1, 2018, will be remembered as the day the American Petroleum Institute (API) caused the Bureau of Ocean Energy Management (BOEM) to award petroleum exploration rights to a number of Outer Continental Shelf (OCS) seismic research groups to commence activities beyond Georgia's 3-mile ocean boundary. Any petroleum corporation that acquires the results of such studies may drill exploration wells in concessions delineated by the BOEM for five years. If successful exploration wells are drilled, development permits will be awarded to the corporation to develop an oilfield by drilling numerous production wells for the life of the field. As a retired petroleum engineer with the largest publicly owned petroleum corporation in the world,

The American Legacy of an Italian Motorcyclist

I feel compelled to share my knowledge about such activities with every individual or group who will be affected by those exploration or production activities.

In April 2010, British Petroleum Corp (BP) drilled a disastrous exploration well off the Louisiana coast. The U.S. Department of Justice (DOJ), after an intensive investigation, found that the "Macondo" blew out due to "deliberate misconduct and gross negligence, causing the worst industrial accident in U.S. history." That blowout could have been prevented but caused 11 immediate drilling crew deaths; 5 million barrels of crude oil contaminating five Gulf Coast states' shores; three years of ineffective shoreline cleanups; continuing impacts on Gulf Coast industries, private enterprises, properties; thousands of marine and avian animals deaths; and over $65 billion in fines.

A new bureau within the Department of the Interior (DOI), the Bureau of Safety & Environmental Enforcement (BSEE) was established in 2011 to establish enforceable rules and practices which might avoid repetitions of BP-like disasters. Since then, an average of four safety-related drafts per year have been proposed, via the API, to the industry. Such is the lobbying power and money of the API that it essentially has captured the BSEE. Numerous national and state organizations have gone on record to criticize the DOI, down to the level of its BSEE, for yielding to

3. ATTACK ON GEORGIA'S COAST

the API rather than developing common sense stringent and enforceable practices. However, if the API claims a BSEE proposed rule requires regular periodic field testing of the critical "tool of last resort," the so-called blowout preventer (BOP), that rule is determined "inconvenient and/or excessively costly," the BSEE backs down and waters down the wording of the rule.

Vote against any politician who supports OCS seismic exploration, which is the first step leading to drilling and development infrastructure.

The American Legacy of an Italian Motorcyclist

4. $66 BILLION AND COUNTING

—Robert Paredi, January 14, 2019

I recently checked to determine the fines levied against the major participants in the infamous "Deep-Water Horizon" (DWH) oil exploration project of 2010, off the Louisiana coast. The Department of Justice (DOJ) declared it to be "the worst industrial accident in U.S. history; caused by deliberate misconduct & gross negligence." The number was $65 *billion*. The amount has risen to $66 billion and counting.

Other findings were called to my attention by Mr. David Hilzenrath, former investigative reporter with *The Washington Post* and now with the nonprofit Project on Government Oversight (POGO), who recently published "When Hell Breaks Over," his exhaustive investigation available online. I highly recommend it to your readers, particularly those skeptical of the motives of ocean conservation organizations, environmentalists, and individuals like myself who have bona fide credentials in petroleum engineering and geology. We oppose our federal administration's hell-bent actions to open petroleum exploration off the Georgia coastline. It's a credit to the SMN in publishing my letters that Mr. Hilzenrath found me. During a lengthy phone call he reviewed his report with me, determining my opinion about details supporting his conclusions. I supported all of them and only offered a few additional discoveries I made recently that reinforced his conclusions. It is an immense credit to our U.S. free press and reporters like David Hilzenrath, who can fearlessly delve into the truth of how our government agencies behave under the relentless pressure and limitless financial resources from major industries' representatives and lobbyists.

Outrageous decisions by the Department of the Interior's (DOI) units such as the Bureau of Ocean Resources & Management (BOEM) and its Bureau of Safety & Environmental Enforcement (BSEE) are exemplified by two examples. By May of 2014, BP had 11 more drilling vessels, similar to the Transocean DWH vessel, conducting exploration drilling. Taylor Corp. erected a flimsy steel-trussed production platform collecting crude oil from 22 wells. In 2004, Hurricane Ivan toppled this platform, leading to the continuous release of

4. $66 BILLION AND COUNTING

crude oil approaching 4m bbls. Taylor declared bankruptcy and inability to pay for the well's abandonment. The company subsequently sold its production rights to a Korean corporation, which has no intention or capability to clean up or contain the ongoing leakage.

Recent executive orders hastening approvals of outer continental shelf Atlantic coast petroleum exploration must be taken seriously. Exert pressure on your politicians! Join the actions of our neighboring states that believe in protecting their shorelines.

The American Legacy of an Italian Motorcyclist

5. THE FIELD OF NIGHTMARES

—Robert Paredi, February 25, 2019

A Consumer Energy Alliance (CEA) lobbyist recently lauded U.S. Representative Buddy Carter's support of the administration's decision to open the outer continental shelf (OCS) to petroleum development. CEA's intention was to apply *The Field of Dreams* movie's message "build it and they will come" to OCS activity beyond our coast. In my opinion this is laughable, misleading, potentially dangerous, and totally disingenuous. If a safe and successful exploration project were to lead to the development of an economically justifiable production facility, an entirely different plethora of pollution sources would appear. They would be protracted, lasting the life of the production facility, possibly beyond. They would be a long-term existential threat to our pristine coast, ocean

351

environment, real estate, coastal tourism, and related industries.

My petroleum engineering career started on Venezuela's Lake Maracaibo. My employer out-produced all others and had the world's largest private navy, with all manner of supporting facilities. Having mastered Spanish, I was once assigned to accompany a Venezuelan government official on twice-weekly helicopter surveys over our concessions to observe and estimate the barrels of crude oil slicks floating downwind, polluting the lake shores. For example, the inspector would estimate 100 barrels. I would counter with 20 barrels and sign off on 50 barrels. The sources were different and numerous. Yearly high-level meetings were held between my corporation and Venezuelan officials. The meetings covered many topics, including the magnitude of fines we were levied based upon the annual volume of crude polluting the lake shore. I subsequently was directed to make a detailed examination of all sources of such contamination. I was quite pleased with my detailed findings of X-number of barrels. My boss commended my report's thoroughness but nothing was done. The penalty fines were cheaper than improving the maintenance operation.

The development phase of any production complex comprises multitudes of producing wells, submarine pipelines, production platforms loading tankers and/or pumping volumes of crude to coastal tank-farms. Such infrastructure, including refineries, exists all along the ocean fronts of the Gulf Coast, California, and Alaska. Only the federal government has benefited from associated royalties. While those states gained employment from the petroleum industry, they achieved those "gains" at the cost of ruined beaches and impaired tourism facilities and revenues. Development will pollute our unique coastline.

DON'T BUILD IT AND THEY WON'T COME!

The American Legacy of an Italian Motorcyclist

6. "ALL OF THE ABOVE" IS NO GOOD

—Robert Paredi, April 1, 2019

The Consumer Energy Alliance (CEA) encourages Georgia's U.S. Rep. Buddy Carter's efforts to support exploration of all Georgia's possible energy sources. The latter include fossil fuels (coal, oil, gas) and renewable solar and wind sources. The CEA even uses the theme "build it and they will come" from the Hollywood movie *The Field of Dreams* to support the notion. The actual result were oil reserves to be produced from the Outer Continental Shelf (OCS, from 3 to 200 miles beyond our beaches), would more than likely result in an "Oil-field of Nightmares."

The production phase of an oilfield follows a successful exploration phase of seismic surveys and drilling of many hazardous exploration wells. It inevitably leads to the installation of a vast complex of submarine and terrestrial equipment transporting a basically filthy and dangerous product. Visualize hundreds or more wellheads on the ocean floor connected by pipelines to submarine manifolds connecting to production platforms (PPs) floating on the surface or erected on flimsy towers planted upon the ocean floor. PPs are the size of football fields, housing oil and gas separators, measuring devices, storage tanks, huge reciprocating pumps loading crude onto tankers, and/or shore-bound tank-farms surrounded by dikes to contain leakages. Finally, pumping stations and pipelines are constructed onshore to deliver crude to refineries.

All the above components can and do leak in spite of considerable effort and maintenance expenses. The U.S. Coast Guard flies over the ocean downwind of the field to locate oil-slicks and estimate the volume of leaked crude drifting on the ocean. Fines are levied on the operator commensurate to the leak. The operator pays the insignificant fines, compared to the impossible task of maintaining a perfectly leak-less mechanical infrastructure and the market value of the product. Prevailing east winds blow crude upon Georgia's pristine beaches, resorts, real estate, polluting everything in its path, including fisheries, marshes, and oyster farms. All such Georgia private, commercial, government, and industrial properties and activities will be affected.

6. "ALL OF THE ABOVE" IS NO GOOD

Taylor Energy (TE) lost a flimsily supported PP to Hurricane Ivan in 2004, 4 years before the catastrophic BP exploration blowout, collecting crude from 28 wells at 450 feet ocean depth. "Ivan" simultaneously triggered a submarine avalanche covering the wellheads. TE declared bankruptcy, thereby avoiding financial responsibility to locate and properly abandon the wells, which leak to this day.

We must prevent such disasters from polluting Georgia's coast!

The American Legacy of an Italian Motorcyclist

7. THANKS TO REP. CARTER

—Robert Paredi, May 3, 2019

The federal government's precipitous initiation of offshore petroleum exploration and development triggered statewide opposition from Georgians. We have pristine islands, vast marshes, abundant wildlife—including commercial and recreational fisheries, and North Atlantic Right Whales. Coastal communities, tourism, and related industries contribute 23,000 jobs and $1.3 B of annual GDP to Georgia's economy.

Recently Georgia's opposition boomed. Fifteen municipalities in Georgia passed resolutions opposing offshore drilling and were joined by five more in this first quarter. Recently, Georgia's House of Representatives passed a resolution opposing offshore seismic surveys and drilling. Newly elected Governor Kemp frequently stated his

The American Legacy of an Italian Motorcyclist

opposition to offshore petroleum exploration beyond Georgia's coast. Our governor, Georgia's House of Representatives, coastal municipalities, and countless local Georgia residents oppose petroleum exploration. U.S. Representative Buddy Carter sent an official statement to the administration to remove Georgia from the Five-Year Plan for Oil and Gas leasing off Georgia. Together, the voices of our state leaders, local city leaders, and countless residents have been heard, and Rep. Carter carried them all the way to D.C.

Representative Carter's official statement should not go unnoticed. Why? Because Mr. Carter personally supports offshore drilling. Nonetheless, he finally accepts his responsibility to adopt his constituents' opposition to the reckless and hell-bent federal program. "While I will continue to be an ardent supporter of American energy independence, I believe that the will of our state and local communities must be respected in a decision of this magnitude. That is why I want to bring to your attention a resolution that overwhelmingly passed in the Georgia House of Representatives this week opposing offshore energy development off Georgia's coast. The resolution passed in the legislature this week was preceded by the approval of resolutions opposing offshore energy development by several municipalities." Representative Carter made the right decision. He has earned the recognition and thanks of many people and organizations working hard to convince him of the threat of the petroleum industry and a compliant administration. Environmental activist organizations including OCEANA, "One Hundred Miles," the Ocean Conservancy, and many others no doubt contributed to the groundswell of resistance which helped him arrive at this very positive and extremely important conclusion.

Thanking Rep. Carter and the environmentally active organizations in this moment of unity is an important step in maintaining opposition to the oil industry and its federal partners. We must now keep pressure upon the federal offices and agencies to ensure that offshore seismic and drilling activities never come to Georgia's coast.

Update: December 2020

Representative Carter showed his true colors in late 2020, supporting the Trump administration's policy on offshore oil exploration in the Atlanta Ocean's Outer Continental Shelf beyond our Eastern Seaboard states.

The American Legacy of an Italian Motorcyclist

8. DOI PECCADILLO

—Robert Paredi, June 3, 2019

David Bernhardt, the new Secretary of the Department of the Interior (DOI) and a well-known lobbyist with the American Petroleum Institute (API), gifted it with a new rule about testing blow-out preventers (BOPs), a critical oil well safety device. One failed to prevent the Deepwater Horizon blowout in 2010. The lawsuit adjudicated by the Department of Justice (DOJ) found British Petroleum (BP) and co-defendants guilty of "Deliberate misconduct and gross negligence in causing the worst industrial accident in American history." Eleven drilling crew workers were instantly cremated alive in the catastrophe, millions of barrels of crude oil contaminated Gulf waters for five months, and significant loss of wildlife was documented.

363

The American Legacy of an Italian Motorcyclist

A new organization, maladroitly titled the "Bureau of Safety & Environmental Enforcement" (BSEE) was established. Its mission statement requires it to issue enforceable rules over petroleum industry operations in exploratory and development oil well drilling. The Obama administration established the BSEE two years after the BP catastrophe after discovering that no such agency had ever existed. The BSEE has proceeded to draft an average of five drilling safety rules annually, posting them in the Federal Register for comment. Every such rule was substantially reworded by the API, rendering it useless in supporting the BSEE mission statement. The DOI announcement of the new rule, developed by the BSEE, was touted as an "improvement." This is an outright misrepresentation of the new rule, which materially negates the prior rule, neither of which was or will be enforceable.

Voters and politicians who support petroleum exploration in Atlantic waters should realize that "it's the wild west out there," and the fox in the hen house is the API fed by the BSEE. DOJ fines of 66 billion dollars in the BP blowout are apparently considered inconsequential by the petroleum industry and won't change its behavior!

Update to letter #8:

This letter, when written in June 2019, disclosed the malevolent practice of the president of the

364

8. DOI PECCADILLO

United States at the time to appoint individuals from prominent lobbying organizations to head up cabinet level positions bearing the responsibility for overseeing the very industries from which they originated. Mr. David Bernhardt, of the American Petroleum Institute, earlier that year had been appointed by the POTUS as Secretary of the Department of The Interior. The DOI oversees the Bureau of Offshore Energy Management, which in turn oversees the recently established Bureau of Safety and Environmental Enforcement. Under Mr. Bernhardt's direction both the BOEM and BSEE methodically proceeded to rescind directives in draft or actually previously approved which would have improved safety procedures and equipment. The API, arguably the largest and most powerful lobbying body in the world and financed by the American petroleum industry, proceeded to direct its two bureaus to cease proposing any rules which would require compliance or be enforced upon its subject industries or corporations. Any previously approved measures directed at managerial responsibilities or equipment design or operational procedures were to be rewritten avoiding any inference of enforcement, penalty for non-compliance, or fines. The API is the most influential organization that reviews all proposed drafts of standards or guidelines appearing in the Government Register having to do with the U.S. oil industry. The new litmus test in determining if a proposal is accepted or not: is it deemed "too

365

expensive or too inconvenient"? For instance, if the operational testing of a blowout preventer during a well drilling procedure requires periodic testing at shift change, daily, weekly, or monthly intervals, the proposal would be deemed "too expensive or inconvenient." The BSEE would reword the draft until it was accepted by the API. The BOP is the most relied upon, most expensive, and most complicated piece of equipment, whether mounted atop the wellhead of valves on the ground or at the bottom of the sea in marine operations.

The BOP is ill-advisedly relied upon by drill crews and their managers to protect them and activate itself automatically and without fail. It should detect a blowout-in-the-making in the wellbore thousands of feet downhole before the drill crew members on the rig floor realize what is in store for them.

9. LET THE OIL STAY THERE

—Robert Paredi, August 2, 2019

Consumer Energy Alliance (CEA) is not an alliance of consumers. It's an alliance of many petroleum industries, including Exxon-Mobil, Shell, BP, Chevron, and even Statoil, the Norwegian petroleum industry! CEA is a front group for an international coalition of oil industries opposing efforts to regulate carbon standards while advancing deep water exploration and development all over the world. Its Atlanta office has had letters published in the SMN.

Poorly understood by the public, and many in Congress, are the details of petroleum concession awards process managed by the Department of Interior's (DOI) Bureau of Ocean Energy Management (BOEM). It maps and defines 25 square mile sections/concessions of the ocean floor beyond all adjoining ocean-bordering states' boundaries. Beyond all those boundaries the U.S. Federal Government has total control to 200 miles terminating at international ocean waters. There would be approximately 400 concessions of 25 square miles each beyond Georgia waters defined by the BOEM.

The "5-year Plan" of the DOI would expedite the concession-award process by immediately launching environmentally damaging seismic surveys whose results are available to petroleum industries bidding for exclusive rights to drill dangerous exploratory wells: "wildcats." This phase would determine the existence, scope, depth, and quality of oil- and gas-bearing strata within corporations' concessions. Within five years of their concession award, corporations could determine to extend their concession's rights and develop the vast infrastructure of production equipment including wells, pipelines, production platforms, storage tanks, shore-based tank farms, large-diameter pipelines, networks of pumping stations, refineries, and shipping facilities. Leaks will carry ashore, 24/7, driven by prevailing winds; corporations will easily pay the fines because leakages are impossible to prevent.

Our congressional rep has said, "I don't think anything is out there but I would like to know." We must assume there is something out there, and it must stay there.

10. SUBSIDENCE, THE SLEEPING GIANT

—Robert Paredi, September 1, 2019

Underground geologic phenomena of collapsing oil-
and gas-bearing strata of oilfields are called
subsidence. Entrained gas in petroleum "reservoir"
fluid (oil, gas, water) at high pressure is the motive
force which drives fluids to the surface. The
production phase of an oilfield launches
subsidence because the undisturbed pressurized
reservoir fluid had prevented the earth from
collapsing. As entrained gas is produced with its
crude oil, support of the overlying earth begins
diminishing. Productive lives of oilfields can last
more than a century until the bulk of their
economically retrievable oil is produced. For the
oilfield's life, the sinking of the earth proceeds
unrelentingly from every well to neighboring areas
in terrestrial or marine environments. Wells and

surface equipment are damaged, as are properties at great distances from the oilfield.

Venezuelan oilfields beneath Lake Maracaibo produced for decades before I arrived in the late '50s. Our 4000 flowing and pumped wells caused the lake bottom and surrounding terrain to sink about 15 feet; a lengthy dike prevented lake waters from flooding the "low country" where we lived. The parking lot at our HQ office flagpole had a tape around it 15 feet above the pavement marking the lake water level beyond the dike within walking distance. Square miles of facilities, including warehouses, shopping centers, industrial complexes, and suburbs were protected by that dike.

Subsidence has occurred for years adjacent to all U.S. oilfields, both terrestrial and marine. Recent news coverage reports subsidence-caused damage to Louisiana marshland, adjacent cities; homeowners being forced to relocate to preserve their livelihoods and protect their families.

This part of Georgia is known as the "low country." If you want Georgia to look like coastal Louisiana or the eastern shore of Lake Maracaibo, continue to support our elected congressman who has stated he "would like to know what's out there."

I don't.

11. WE MUST PROTECT OUR SHORES

—Robert Paredi, November 15, 2019

U.S. coastlines and economies are being threatened. Offshore seismic exploration is deadly to marine creatures, and lead to five years of exploration drilling of dangerous "wildcat wells." Bipartisan coast-to-coast opposition to dirty and dangerous offshore seismic and drilling exploration must prevent the permanent loss of more than 23,000 Georgia jobs and $1.3 billion annually from fishing, tourism, and recreational revenues. Across the U.S., offshore seismic surveys followed by exploration drilling threaten 2.6 million jobs and $180 billion in GDP.

I was invited to join and participate with a delegation of 29 OCEANA supporters from California to Maine on November 12 to Capitol Hill. OCEANA's "fly-in" was an extremely well-organized lobbying project by OCEANA's DC Headquarters to oppose offshore seismic and exploration drilling funds being included in the 2020 federal funding bill. In 60 meetings with members of Congress, the delegation emphasized the risks that such a program would impose upon our coastal states' economies and citizens.

The present administration is hell-bent on pursuing an aggressive program further benefiting the U.S. petroleum industry at a time when the U.S. has proven petroleum reserves of 90 years at present consumption, including export requirements, the embargo of which was lifted years ago. Our existing petroleum industry is certainly a critical resource that will continue to satisfy the needs of our aviation industry and military requirements, particularly since the 90-year reserves figure is predicted to increase without prospective petroleum developments in the U.S. Outer Continental Shelf. Global climate realities demand that the implacable market growth of clean energy sources must be recognized by our administration and encouraged by new, rational national energy policies.

Don't believe fallacious arguments presented by the petroleum industry, its supporters, and prominent federal officials who ignore and ridicule the rapidly growing market-driven demands and supply of clean and renewable energy.

11. WE MUST PROTECT OUR SHORES

Update to letter #11

TESLA Corp., the American electric vehicle manufacturer, announced in 2020 that it would relocate its vehicle manufacturing and electric battery production facilities from California to Texas. These market-driven decisions exemplify how proximity to the Texas electrical grid with its relatively less expensive supply of electricity, generated by a growing supply of renewable energy, attracted TESLA. A growing segment of renewable energy sources (solar and wind) took place in the face of a hostile federal government. In the absence of the Texas electrical grid, it's doubtful that this decision would have been taken by TESLA. The new U.S. administration, as of January 2021, has signaled that it will support future development of additional domestic renewable energy sources. Such progressive industrial energy infrastructure development is essential to pursue the aggressive support of U.S. actions to confront global warming and climate change phenomena consistent with the goals of the worldwide Paris Climate Accord.

The intention of the new U.S. administration to rejoin the PCA's 194 worldwide governmental units is essential to demonstrate that the U.S. believes the scientific community. More importantly, "protecting our shores," while sounding like a purely nationalistic pursuit, cannot be accomplished without protecting the world's shores. The U.S. is certainly not the only nation suffering the oceanic and atmospheric ravages of climate change and ocean warming. Other purely "America only" national projects, such as modernizing and repairing our infrastructure (roads, bridges, dams, electrical generating plants), must include the modernization of our two major electrical eastern and western electrical grids, recognized as being in poor repair, obsolescent, and limited in national coverage. This latter opportunity has huge potential to broaden our manufacturing base into our central basin states, with attendant significant new job growth in those areas.

12. OYSTERS & OIL DON'T MIX

—Robert Paredi, November 19, 2019

Oyster aficionados are heartened to see prospective oyster farmers attempting to establish oyster farming along our sea-front. They appreciate how their objectives depend upon preservation of Georgia's pristine seafront and estuaries.

The aggressive federal program to launch exploration and development of Atlantic Offshore Continental Shelf (OCS) 200 miles beyond our 3-mile state waters pose existential threats to marine industries and oceanic life, from whales and turtles to micro-organisms beneath our seashore and marshes. Oysters are filter-feeders, each gleaning food by constantly pumping so many gallons per day of seawater, obtaining food of aquatic organisms and ejecting "purified" seawater.

The American Legacy of an Italian Motorcyclist

Unnecessary development of petroleum resources off our Atlantic OCS, given that the U.S. presently has 90 years of proven crude-oil reserves for its domestic and export market, suggests that those OCS probable crude-oil reservoirs need not be explored or developed. The oil industry is vital to our security and critical military and civil industrial needs. The U.S. market-growth of non-fossil fuels is accelerating and will exploit a significant supply of "clean and renewable energy" for our domestic civilian market. Therefore, our Atlantic states mustn't sacrifice their pristine coasts, impairing their existing industries, tourism, commercial and private properties.

After the catastrophic 2010 BP "Deep Water Horizon" blowout, the U.S. Coast Guard attempted to burn and sink the ensuing 5 million barrels of crude leakage slick. Approx. 1.8 million gallons of the controversial surfactant COREXIT were sprayed, sinking the film to the ocean bottoms and marshes; this made the droplets 52 times more toxic to sub-marine organisms than the crude itself. An Oklahoma-sized sea-bottom also became devoid of life.

The trickle-effect of imperfect OCS-based oil facilities' maintenance would definitely lead to a constant crude-oil wind and tidally delivered poisonous slick upon our coastal marine biosphere. That would imperil much more than the oysters.

13. *GOLDEN RAY* SALVAGE CHALLENGE

—Robert Paredi, April 19, 2020

On Sept. 8, 2019, the roll-on, roll-off vehicle transport ship *Golden Ray* capsized, loaded with 4,200 new Hyundai & Kia vehicles outbound 23 minutes from its departure around midnight from the Port of Brunswick bound for Baltimore Port.

The ship's 24 tanks were loaded with 320,000 gallons of bunker fuel and every vehicle with diesel or gasoline fuel, lubricants and antifreeze. The vehicles were parked, unsecured, on 11 decks below the main deck. Twenty-three crewmen plus the Altamaha River Pilot were aboard when a fire reportedly occurred in the engine room. The pilot immediately steered the boat off the federal outbound ship channel onto the shallow river bank causing the 660-foot ship to capsize onto its port side.

The ship remains at that spot and its salvage completion date recently postponed to August, missing the June 1 start of hurricane season by two months. The project proceeds under a "unified command" comprising the U.S. Coast Guard, Georgia Department of Natural Resources and the salvage project contractor.

The critically important Environmental Protection Barrier, or EPB, surrounds the wreck within 33 acres of pilings that support an underwater steel and fabric mesh of 5-feet-by-5-feet square openings. It collects miscellaneous mechanical debris caused by the diamond-studded cutting chain that takes only 24 hours to cut through the ship's hull to remove tanks and vehicles at seven locations. The vehicles, fuel tank pieces and other debris will be captured by the EPB before it can drift downstream or upstream in the 4- to 6-knot current caused by tidal rising and reversing in St. Simons Sound. Oil slicks are supposedly intercepted by absorbent fabric-coated booms attached to the upper edges of the EPB.

Early in the project oil slicks evaded the booms and were discovered by fishermen south of the project; 30 miles of St. Simons Sound, island beaches and estuaries were contaminated.

Northeastern Florida communities get this news. Why don't we?

13. GOLDEN RAY SALVAGE CHALLENGE

Update to letter #13

The pursuit of the salvage operation of the GOLDEN RAY *automobile transport ship continues far behind schedule and presently risks missing the start of Georgia's hurricane season for the second year in 2021. Fortunately, there have been no casualties to the salvage operation's large 24 hours/day operating staff or project monitoring personnel. The ongoing unique and complex hull cutting operation proceeds with several of 7 sections of the still-loaded hull, which contains 4200 new vehicles, having been removed and shipped to salvage facilities. Continuous monitoring of petroleum products escaping from the surrounding floating containment system has been successful in preventing serious environmental degradation of adjacent shorelines. Periodic reports, including live photography of the hazardous activities of salvage staff, are available to the public.*

The American Legacy of an Italian Motorcyclist

14. FOSSIL FUEL INDUSTRY SKEWS CLEAN INDUSTRY FACTS

—Robert Paredi, March 23, 2021

The new U.S. administration's rejoining the Paris Climate Accord acknowledges that single countries cannot solve the climate problem by themselves. The market-driven growth of renewable energy sources—solar and wind—is a direct threat to fossil fuel industries. As long as a particular oil corporation's annual dividends satisfy its investors, its chief executive can relax.

The word "institute" in the American Petroleum Institute (API) title implies an organization having a scientific, educational, or social purpose. The API is nothing of the sort. It is predominantly an organization of oil industry executives and professional employees of every U.S. oil corporation. Its purpose is simply to protect and enhance its members' independence from government oversight and the imposition of enforceable rules that might increase its cost of doing business. One such safety rule was directed at blowout preventers; the API immediately vetoed it since it was declared "too inconvenient or expensive" to accept.

Fines levied by the Coast Guard for ocean oil slicks caused by leaking mechanical equipment, crude oil wellheads or submarine pipelines damaged by corrosion are paid to adjoining states if the offending corporation considers the fines to be less expensive than preventive measures to improve maintenance. Indeed, our previous administration had aggressively been removing and loosening environmental protection and safety measures affecting the oil industry.

Clean energy devices are inherently non-polluting, and more cost-competitive than fossil fuels while not contributing to ocean warming or climate change. The API must resist the temptation to support or originate spurious claims to the contrary.

Additional Resources

David Hilzenrath, Investigative Journalist with Project on Government Oversight (POGO), Washington, D.C. As a reporter for *The Washington Post,* Mr. Hilzenrath reported on the Deepwater Horizon "worst industrial accident in U.S. History" and with POGO published a three-part series on the hazards of offshore drilling and the Bureau of Safety and Environmental Enforcement's effort to loosen safety requirements for blowout preventers. Go to David Hilzenrath, Chief Investigative Reporter, POGO, 240-304-7264 (mobile), 202-347-1122

www.pogo.org/dhilzenrath@pogo.org/@DavidHilzenrath

Rachel Maddow is the author of *BLOWOUT,* "the story of the richest, most destructive industry on earth," and host of the eponymous MSNBC TV editorial weeknight program offering insightful review and analysis of U.S. "breaking news."

OCEANA, the worldwide 501.c3 organization dedicated to science-based reporting on the health of the worldwide oceans, their aquatic animal populations' health, marshes and reef conditions, impacts of industrial activities on sea-life, lobbying activities to promote governmental oversight, and legislative activities supporting environmental protection of oceanic resources. Founded in 2001, it is the largest international advocacy organization focused solely on ocean conservation.

Go to http://ow.ly/HoEaH

Photo credits

With exceptions as noted below, all illustrations are from the collection of Robert J. Paredi.

Page 92. Map of San Francisco and its environs courtesy of GalliBM Own Work Previously published: www.sfbaywatertrail.org.

Page 224. Map of Lake Maracaibo courtesy of en.wikipedia.org.

Page 233. Map of the Orinoco River basin courtesy of biofreshblog.com

Page 273. Map of Norway courtesy of nationsonline.org.

Front cover:

Nino Paredi, pausing to smoke a cigarette astride his Indian motorcycle, not far from the front lines. Note the polished, knee-high boots. "Indian" is legible, if faint, on the gas tank.

The American Legacy of an Italian Motorcyclist

Nino's Croix de Guerre medal, World War I

San Francisco's Golden Gate Bridge, chrome postcard, published sometime in the 1950s

Derrick and Creole Corp. tank, Venezuela, chrome postcard, postmarked 1964

Back cover:

The author, Bob Paredi

Background: San Francisco's Market Street, real photo postcard, circa the 1930s or thereabouts

Made in the USA
Columbia, SC
30 April 2021